PENSION HANDBOOK

FOR UNION NEGOTIATORS

PENSION HANDBOOK

FOR UNION NEGOTIATORS

Jeffrey A. MacDonald
Senior Staff Associate
George Meany Center for Labor Studies

and

Anne Bingham
Managing Editor
International Union,
Allied Industrial Workers of America, AFL-CIO

The Bureau of National Affairs, Inc.
Washington, D.C.

Library of Congress Cataloging-in-Publication Data

MacDonald, Jeffrey A.
  Pension handbook for union negotiators.

  Includes index.
  1. Pensions—United States. 2. Pension trusts—United States.
I. Bingham, Anne. II. Title.
HD7125.M28 1986   331.25′2′0973   85-29959
ISBN 0-87179-479-9

Printed in the United States of America
International Standard Book Number 0-87179-479-9

Introduction

This book is a "how to" guide to negotiating the single-employer, private sector pension plan. It is intended to provide a useful general introduction to the subject of pensions as well as practical help in preparing for and negotiating contracts. The book should prove especially useful for local union officers and bargaining committee members, business agents and representatives with responsibilities for several local unions, and regional and international union staff involved in the pension area.

Public sector pensions and multiemployer plans are sufficiently different from single-employer, private sector plans to require a depth of discussion beyond the scope of this book. Therefore, these topics are not covered in detail.

Pension Handbook for Union Negotiators concentrates on giving the reader a good understanding of how a pension works, what the various terms found in pension agreements mean, how to achieve desired pension goals, and what to expect at the bargaining table. The last chapter of this book contains a limited set of goals for pension negotiators. These goals reflect the opinions of the authors and do not necessarily reflect the position of either the Allied Industrial Workers of America, AFL-CIO, or the George Meany Center for Labor Studies.

The book is intended to be practical, leaving it to others to consider any broad social and economic questions. It does not address the question of what constitutes an adequate pension benefit because, as a practical matter, no union negotiator has ever encountered one. There's always room for improvement.

It must also be kept in mind that pensions represent, after all, only a small part of the labor movement's collective effort to establish and maintain economic security for its members. The rest of the picture includes such efforts as working on bills to improve Social Security or Medicare; giving testimony for or against changes in workers' compensation laws; serving on community boards of public

service agencies, and so on. Amid all this activity the union negotiator is just another piece of the puzzle—an important piece to be
sure, but not the only one.

This patchwork of private, public, individual, and collective
action is mostly an ad hoc, uncoordinated response to the aging of
America over the past century. Our society has grown older both in
absolute and relative terms. Medical advances, reduced family size,
and fewer immigrants all have played a part in the process; this
change occurred while our economic system went from a primarily
agricultural to a primarily industrial system. As people moved from
the country to smaller houses in the city, as families became smaller
and people became less rooted to their home towns, care for an
increasingly older population became more difficult. Most afford-
able homes today just don't have room for three generations under
one roof.

Labor's attitude toward retirement income has undergone a
change as well. Before the Depression, unions viewed pensions not
as a desirable benefit but as a management ploy to prevent unioniza-
tion. Because few laws regulated pensions prior to the 1930s, an
employer's threat that workers would lose their pensions if they
formed a union was very real. Further, unions were sufficiently
preoccupied just obtaining a living wage for working members that
the problems of retired workers received relatively little attention.
The frontier ethic of rugged individualism was still strong; the
prevailing attitude was that workers would provide for their own
retirement if they received an adequate wage. Those who didn't
were considered shiftless.

The frontier ethic began to crack during the 1930s. The view
that the individual was solely responsible for his or her own economic well-being came into clear conflict with the realities of a
modern industrial society. Poverty on the scale caused by the
Depression obviously could not be blamed on a few shiftless individuals. Accordingly, the belief grew that society had a responsibility for the individual welfare of its members, especially in their old
age. The Social Security Act of 1935 was one result.

At this time the labor movement hoped that Social Security
benefits would eventually rise high enough to be the sole source of
retirement income. The first pension agreements therefore tied
private retirement benefits to the public scheme, calling for a fixed
retirement benefit of $100 a month, including Social Security.
While there were many reasons for this approach, a major one was to
provide corporate America an incentive to join with the labor move-

ment in pressing for higher Social Security benefits. Bigger Social Security checks for workers would mean less for the company to pay in benefits.

However, by the mid-1940s, it was apparent that the changes in society mentioned earlier were making it impossible for even significantly higher Social Security benefits to ensure a secure retirement. Further, wages were rising rapidly enough that unions could turn their attention to other concerns, including private pensions. There sprang up at this time a retirement theory called the "three-legged stool" approach, so named because it was based on individual savings, Social Security, and private pensions. If any one of its "legs" fell off, the system would come tumbling down.

Unfortunately, one of the legs of the stool has always been a bit short, and that's the savings leg. Our economic system experiences high unemployment and high inflation with some amount of regularity; along with this, as a society we heavily consume goods and services. It should then come as no surprise that many people arrive at retirement with little or no savings.

The pension leg was steadied in the early 1970s by the enactment of the Employee Retirement Income Security Act (ERISA), which remedied structural deficiencies and institutional abuses in the pension system. That added support, however, does not help the substantial number of workers still not covered by a pension.

The third leg, Social Security benefits, while certainly the most dependable of the three, is subjected to regular and frequently well-orchestrated attacks, especially when the time comes to adjust the funding.

In short, the reality of retirement income security is far less certain than the three-legged stool analogy would indicate. In recent years the stool has been further destabilized by a resurgent focus, harking back to the pre-Depression emphasis on the rugged individual, on the individual saver. This time, however, the government is the source behind the focus, by providing tax breaks to people with Individual Retirement Accounts, and Keogh plans (retirement accounts for the self-employed). While it's difficult to criticize any kind of savings plan—it's like being against apple pie—the long-term effects of this new emphasis on individual savings look ominous to some pension watchers. What effect will the emphasis on individual savings have on the constituency that supports Social Security? On private pension reform? No one knows at this point, but it's certain that the problem is far from resolved today. The struggle now is just as important as it was 10, 20, even 50 years ago.

Contents

Introduction v

1. The Unique Fringe Benefit 1

   Economic Security 2
   Size of the Problem 3
   The Role of Time 4
   Effect of the Economy 6

2. Government's Role in Pension Administration 8

   Qualified Pension Plan 9
   Funding 10
   The Actuary 10
   The Trustee 11
   The Federal Government 12
      National Labor Relations Act 12
      ERISA and the Pension Contract 15
         Participation 16
         Vesting 16
         Definition of Hours and Years of Service 16
         Statutory Joint and Survivor Option at
            Retirement 17
         Preretirement Spousal Coverage 17
         Plan Modification and Termination 17
         Dispute Resolution 17
         Participant Information Rights 18
      Pension Benefit Guaranty Corporation 19

3. How a Pension Works 20

   What a Pension Is 20
      A Group Plan 20
      A Savings Plan 21
      A Retirement Income Plan 23

A Dependable Income 23
How Pensions Differ from Other Savings Plans 24
    Income Goals 24
    Participant's Life Expectancy 25
    Effect of Interest on the Needed Lump Sum 26
    How Age Affects Cost 28
    How Interest Rates Affect Cost 28
The Group Aspect of Pensions 29
    Effects of Turnover and Mortality 30
    Actuarial Assumptions and Costs 31
Summary 32

4. **Defined-Benefit and Defined-Contribution Plans** 34

What the Benefit Is 34
How Age Affects the Benefit 35
Individual Versus Group Funding 36
    Advantages of Individual Funding 37
        Simplicity 37
        Immediate Vesting 37
        100 Percent Funding 37
        Portability 37
    Disadvantages of Individual Funding 38
        Expense 38
        Who Bears the Risk 39
        Negligible Credit for Past Service 39
        Disability 40
Hybrid Plans 40
How to Offset the Disadvantages of Defined-
        Contribution Plans 41
    Control Investments 42
    Limit Choice 42
    Ensure Disability Provisions 42
    Take Care of Older Members 42
    Piggyback Plans 42

5. **The Defined-Benefit Plan: Benefits** 43

The Normal Retirement Benefit 44
    Purely Income-Based Formulas 44
    Income and Service Formulas 44
    Flat Dollar and Service Formulas 48
    Flat Dollar Benefits 50
Early Retirement Benefits 50

Actuarial Reduction 50
Health Insurance 54
Social Security Supplement 54
Surviving Spouse Benefits 55
Preretirement Surviving Spouse Coverage 55
Automatic Joint-and-Survivor Coverage 57
Summary 59

6. The Defined Benefit Plan: Language 60

How Pension Language Affects Members 60
Participation 61
Service Accrual 62
Elapsed Time 63
Hours Counting 65
Breaks in Service and Severance from Service 67
Vesting 68
Benefit Eligibility 71
Plan Administration 72
Pension Dispute Resolution 73
Joint Administrative Committees 73
Plan Funding and Investments 74
Plan Amendment 76
Union Rights 77

7. Preparing to Bargain 79

Information the Union Already Has 79
Qualified Pension Plan 79
Amendments to the Qualified Pension Plan 80
Previous Contract Negotiations 80
Information Available Through the Company 81
What the Information Means 83
Data on Active Pension Plan Participants 83
Data on Retired Participants 84
Annual Company Contributions Schedule and
Level of Contributions 84
The Three Most Recent Actuarial Evaluations 85
The Three Latest Department of Labor 5500 Forms . . 85
The Three Latest Trustee Reports 86
Information from Outside Sources 86
Basic Retirement Benefits 87
Pension Language 87
Pension Reporting Services 88

8. **Pension Bargaining Timeline** 90

Choosing and Preparing Proposals 91
   Define Problems 92
   Submit Alternatives 92
   Include Minor Issues 92
   Put It in Writing 93
   Document the Problem 93
   Review Past Negotiations 93
The First Day of Bargaining 93
   How to Highlight Pensions 94
   Allocating Time 94
Language Sessions 96
First Session on Economics 97
Early Counterproposals 97
Final Hours Before the Contract Expires 98
Ratification Meeting and After 99

9. **Pension Bargaining and Costs** 101

Determining the Cost of Current Benefits 102
Finding Cents-per-Hour Worked 102
   Detecting Cost Trends 102
   Interpreting Cost Data 104
Improvements 105
   Estimating the Cost of an Improvement 106
   Variables that Affect the Calculation 107
   Calculating for Percent of Earnings Formulas 108
Early Retirement Benefit Improvements 110
   No-Cost Programs 111
   Programs Involving a Cost to the Plan 111
     Negotiated Modifications 111
     Early Retirement Supplements 114
Disability Pensions 115
Vesting 116
Preretirement Surviving Spouse Provisions 117
Pension Costs and Bargaining Strategy 119
   Focus on Need, not Cost 119
   Avoid Specific Figures 120
Summary 120

10. **Pension Investment Control** 122

Ownership is not Control 122
Why Unions Are Interested in Investment Control 124

Preliminary Decisions 125
Preparing to Bargain 127
Bargaining Strategy 128
What to Negotiate 128

11. **Pension Negotiations During a Plant Closing** 132

When to Negotiate Pension Rights 132
Information the Union Needs to Obtain 133
Responding to the Company's Announcement 134
How the Company Can React 135
Limits on the Company's Right to Terminate 137
The Role of the PBGC 139
Proposals to Make During a Plant Closing 139

12. **Bargaining Agenda for the Future** 143

Agenda for Defined-Benefit Plans 143
Agenda for Defined-Contribution Plans 146

Appendices

A. Components of a Defined-Benefit Plan 149
B. Present Value of $1 Received Annually for
     N Years 150
C. Future Values of an Annuity of $1 151
D. The Effect of Age on Pension Cost 152
E. Mortality Tables—Males 153
F. Pension Costs Adjusted for Mortality and Turnover . . 155
G. Pension Summary Analysis 156
H. Letter Requesting Pension Information
     Held by Company 158
I. Actuarial Assumptions and Cost Method 159
J. Department of Labor 5500 Forms 162
K. Department of Labor 5500 Pension Analysis 172
L. Computing Fringe Benefit Costs 174
M. Sample Language on Joint Control of Pension Plan
     Administration and Investment 178

Glossary 181

Index 185

1

The Unique Fringe Benefit

Negotiating a retirement income plan—a pension—for your members is very different from negotiating other fringe benefits or wages. You're attempting to set up a plan that will provide economic security 10, 20, even 40 years in the future, and you know it's impossible to predict exactly how much money you'll be needing six months from now.

And pensions are complicated. While an hour's study will give you a good understanding of holiday pay, shift differentials, the company's absentee policy, and similar provisions of the bargaining agreement, when you start to study pensions you'll be tempted to either throw in the towel after the first 15 minutes or move into a library for several months. Typical pension documents are lengthy and written in what can only be described as legalese; they have many separate and very important parts, and sometimes fail to define unfamiliar words. Pension financing is unique and involves many outsiders (including bankers, insurance companies, and actuaries) and occasionally even these "experts" get confused.

The good news is that, while pensions are complicated in the sense that they take time and effort to understand, they are not complex in the sense that Euclidian geometry is complex. Anyone who can read and perform basic addition, subtraction, multiplication, division, and percentages can become quite proficient regarding the topic of pensions. This works to your advantage at the bargaining table and within your union as well. Because pensions have the reputation for being so complicated, with a bit of hard work you can become the pension expert in your local, regional, district, or international union. If you know your stuff, management will be asking *you* for advice after a while.

1

Further, their very complexity makes pensions fascinating for those inclined to pursue them. There's always an opportunity to use your wits at the bargaining table, and the pension area is no exception—in fact, there may be more room for creative solutions to difficult problems in pensions than in any other area of bargaining. And in pension negotiations, it's possible for you to make a noticeable difference in the lives of your members.

Economic Security

While economic security is difficult to define, one thing is certain: in any advanced economy there isn't much of it. Even though the American economic system provides well for the majority of its participants most of the time, some of your members will almost certainly face severe personal economic problems at some point in their lives. The plant may shut down and leave them without income. They may be arbitrarily dismissed from work. Or a family member may suffer an illness of extended duration and the treatment may exhaust the family's financial resources.

A union will protect your members from some of these problems through a grievance procedure and a good health insurance policy, but if unplanned economic dislocations don't happen to you, they'll happen to someone you know. Unfortunately, seemingly random economic catastrophes are not aberrations of the economic system; they're permanent and predictable within a sufficiently large pool of workers.

Think of economic security as a dice game in which the odds are stacked so your chance of winning big is infinitely small, your chance of winning enough to get by is highly probable, and the chance that you'll lose everything and never recover is small but significant. Now roll the dice. Do you feel secure as you're throwing them? Of course not; in fact, you would probably refuse to play a game with this type of risk structure. Luckily, that's where unions come in, and contracts, and pensions.

By thumbing through any collective bargaining agreement, the educated reader can pick up the history of the local. In fact, in examining the articles of a collective bargaining agreement you can take any contract clause and, by tracing it back to the beginning, find someone who was seriously injured, physically or financially, because the clause didn't exist at one time. A labor agreement is probably the best single history of the problems that a group of workers have faced over a given period of time at a particular work place.

It shouldn't surprise anyone that a majority of contract clauses deal with some problem related to economic security: prohibitions against arbitrary and unjust discharge or punishment; seniority; limits on temporary transfers to lower-paying jobs; health and safety protections; group life and health insurance; grievance mechanisms to place the strength of the union behind the individual to protect these rights; a pension plan. No matter how different all these clauses appear on the surface, they have one central purpose: more economic security to improve the odds of the economic dice game.

In this general sense, a pension plan is no different from a seniority clause. The general goal is to create, through a contract, a more secure economic world for your members. However, in other ways pensions are different from other aspects of the contract, both in the size of the problem and in the members' understanding of its urgency.

Size of the Problem

Take the example of a new member who is about to start tomorrow as an apprentice welder on the third shift. She's 20 years old. Now this new member is going to face all sorts of problems throughout her work life, most of which will certainly be of more immediate concern than retirement. In fact, if you were to make the mistake of bending her ear about retirement, she would probably think you have a screw loose. However, sooner or later she'll reach an age where she will either be unable to continue working or no longer want to work. From that time she'll need a regular flow of income to live on. How do you determine how much that will be?

Suppose the young welder will be making roughly $20,000 this coming year. You can't expect her to stay at that rate all her life; at a minimum she'll need wage increases equal to price increases just to stay even. A conservative cost-of-living increase would give the welder a 4 percent increase each year for the next 45 years, which would make her annual income at retirement around $116,800.

When she retires, she'll need to replace this income with a combination of savings, Social Security, and pension. Like most people, she will probably have very little in her savings account, so the bulk of the income replacement will come from Social Security and a private pension plan. For the sake of this example, figure that half ($58,400 a year) will come from each. According to the mortality tables, which you'll learn about in Chapter 3, the retired welder will live for about 15 years beyond her retirement date, which means she'll collect roughly $876,000 in pension income, a tidy sum.

Of course, this example is a bit speculative. No one can predict what the world will be like in 45 years, and you could argue the 50-50 split between pension and Social Security, or the fact that a worker needs as much money in retirement as during the earlier years. But these quibbles don't change the concept that it costs a lot of money to provide an individual with adequate retirement income for maybe 20 percent of that person's life. Consequently, after wages, the pension plan is frequently the most expensive section of the collective bargaining agreement.

The Role of Time

Most negotiated benefits are designed to remedy current problems. Health insurance covers the costs of accident or illness; holiday and vacation pay give your members time off from work; weekly sickness and accident benefits replace income lost today due to illness or accident. But pensions are different. They're negotiated today for an event in the distant future. This characteristic of pensions has both advantages and drawbacks.

The biggest advantage is that it gives you the opportunity to plan ahead, to systematically accumulate the money to provide an adequate retirement income for all your members. However, because a pension seems so distant to the average worker, your members might not be too concerned about the issue, especially in a young shop. And if your members are not concerned, you're going to have a hard time convincing management to take the problem seriously. Everyone would rather have income today than tomorrow, a phenomenon called *time preference*. This means that mortgage payments and grocery bills have more immediacy for most people than something that might come up 40 years from now.

Achieving a broad consensus for either a pension plan or pension improvements takes work on the part of the union leadership. Officers and staff who care about the problem of retirement have to go out and sell the idea to the membership. And you have to do it in terms your members can understand. When the United Mine Workers negotiated a $100 a month pension in 1947, John L. Lewis was asked, "Why $100?" He responded that a miner could dream

THE UNIQUE FRINGE BENEFIT 5

about $100 a month, but that it would be hard to work up enthusiasm for a figure like $98.50.

If it's a *30-and-out* program you're trying to initiate (retirement after 30 years' service, regardless of age), appeal to the younger workers on the issue of jobs. They'll be more willing to support this improvement if they realize that the sooner high seniority workers retire, the sooner young workers can bid onto the day shift. Whenever there's a good pension plan you can be sure the union has had leaders committed to the idea of retirement income security and who have taken the time to educate members about its importance. The moral is that, if you expect to establish or improve a pension plan, don't look for a ground swell of popular support—go out and create it yourself. That's what leaders are for.

An associated problem relating to time occurs at the bargaining table, where one of the most common phrases is "show me the problem." If you can't provide evidence of the problem, management is going to wonder why you're talking about it. From its point of view, the whole purpose of bargaining is to solve actual problems, which is difficult enough; why deal with hypothetical ones?

Well, there's no "maybe" about pensions. Retirement income adequacy is not an "if" issue but a "when" issue. It's natural to defer pension problems until they're on top of you, but it's also disastrous.

Here's an example: When your plan was established it contained a *30-year-cap* on service accrual. This means an individual accumulates service towards a pension up to and including the 30th year of employment, and then the monthly pension benefit is frozen. No service is accumulated beyond that point. If the benefit formula calls for a monthly income equal to $10 multiplied by years of service, at the end of 30 years the benefit would be $300 a month ($10 × 30 years). Because the service is capped, that benefit will stay the same even though an individual works 31, or 35, or 45 years.

It has been a time-honored tradition for your local's bargaining committee to submit a proposal calling for elimination of the 30-year-cap. The company has its own tradition of responding: "What's the problem? All your members have less than 30 years. Nobody's affected by the cap yet. We'll deal with it later, when someone reaches it."

If this goes on during every contract negotiation, when the day of reckoning arrives you won't have just one person at the cap—you'll have a number of them, the employees who were hired when the plant originally opened. This particular group of members will have attended every monthly union meeting for the past eight months, screaming for equal pay for equal work (that is, they want their pension credits). And although they didn't raise a peep about the issue during the 29 years they sat through union meetings and contract ratifications (when they bothered to come), suddenly they'll want to know how the union could have been so "negligent" as to allow this cap to go unchallenged. There's your ground swell. What three years earlier had seemed an academic problem will now be painfully real.

The company will take a different tack than it did three years earlier, too. Instead of denying that the problem is current (which is no longer possible), management will now claim that, although you've gotten its attention, the problem will cost too much to resolve in one set of negotiations—after all, there are 30 or more people who have service in excess of 30 years just waiting for the cap to be eliminated so they can retire. Eliminating the cap would give each of them a monthly pension boost of up to $30 over the term of the three-year agreement, a cost the company says it can't absorb just now.

Regardless of the merits of the positions on either side of the table, or the eventual solution, the fact remains that both parties will be in a difficult situation that could have been avoided. Pension issues are easiest to solve when they have no immediate consequences. It's never too early to start addressing problems you can see on the horizon.

Remember to talk with your retirees when you're thinking about ways to improve the pension plan. Unlike other areas of the collective bargaining agreement, people don't learn about pensions from experience. Most union members have a pretty good idea why the job bidding procedure works in one case but not in another, why a particular health care claim was denied, or why they lost holiday pay because they didn't work the day before and the day after a long weekend. Without reading the contract cover to cover, they've learned what's in it through its day-to-day administration. This doesn't work for pensions, though. How the plan actually works might not be discovered unless the bargaining committee stays on top of the situation. People learn about pensions only when they retire; by then it's too late to remedy a bad situation. This puts a great deal of responsibility on the bargaining committee.

Effect of the Economy

Having said all this, it's important to remember that pension improvements are, in the long run, at the mercy of the nation's economy. The government's tendency to deal with inflation through the unemployment fix has significantly lessened the negotiator's power in this area. Even someone with a strong interest in pension improvements will find it difficult to press the issue of retirement income when half the members are laid off, those working have been asked to take a wage freeze, and the company has proposed seniority modifications to improve efficiency. In any given bargaining situation, a union has only so much economic power; in periods of high unemployment, you'll use that power for current problems, not for future ones. This does not change the magnitude of retirement income needs—only your ability to meet them.

The point is that the collective bargaining process has limits to its ability to create retirement income security; at best, any negotiated program is a supplement to, not a replacement for, the major government sponsored program, Social Security. The rest of this book will explore what you can achieve, and how to achieve it, within these limits.

2

Government's Role in Pension Administration

It isn't easy to negotiate pensions without a firm conceptual grounding. In one case, for example, the union rep from the international had learned pensions as she had worked with them, on an unstructured, case-by-case basis. She had picked up most of the basics, had learned in a general way what a fiduciary is, what an actuary does, and what the Employee Retirement Income Security Act (ERISA) covers. But in each negotiation some new wrinkle would show up, and in the current one, local circumstances indicated that it would make sense for the union to try for some control over the investment of the pension money.

The rep had never negotiated this kind of issue before, and there was no time in the middle of negotiations to give it systematic study. She called her boss, and they worked out how to appear as if she knew what she was doing, just to get the ball rolling. She briefed the bargaining committee, and they returned to the table. Things started off well, and after a few minutes she began to relax. Then the company negotiator interrupted to ask if she was talking about a "GIC" or a "bullet."

The rep didn't have the vaguest idea what the company man was talking about (although later she learned they were different investment vehicles), but all those years of negotiating had taught her to think on her feet. After only the briefest of pauses she informed him that, until there was an agreement in principle, there wasn't much point in discussing details like GICs or bullets. Her bluff succeeded, and the discussion returned to the union's role in determining investment policy. So it's possible, although difficult, to negotiate pensions with only a basic understanding of the issues.

But you will be much more effective, not to mention more comfortable, if you have an overview of the institutional and conceptual relationships involved in the typical single-employer, defined-benefit pension plan. In this chapter you'll begin that overview, and the rest of the book will refine the concepts.

As you can see from Appendix A, the union and employer begin the process by negotiating a pension contract. This legal contract can take many different forms, but in general it spells out the amount of income an individual can expect at retirement and the eligibility requirements for receiving that income. The diagram deals with a *defined-benefit* pension contract, which means that the contract promises a specific retirement benefit; there is another kind of pension contract which simply spells out the contribution and which, logically enough, is known as a *defined-contribution* pension. The differences between the two will be covered in Chapters 4 and 5.

Union negotiators are most intensely involved at the point when the terms and conditions of the basic pension contract are negotiated. Chapters 5 and 6 will cover the details of this contract, and Chapters 7 and 8 will cover the actual negotiation.

Qualified Pension Plan

The controlling document for the whole pension planning process is called the *qualified pension plan.* "Qualified" refers to the fact that the company must submit its pension plan and any amendments to the Internal Revenue Service for review to ensure that its terms comply with ERISA and the Internal Revenue Code; only then can the company write off its pension contributions as a business expense.

Despite the qualified pension plan's central importance, it's not unusual for both unions and employers to be confused about what it is, or even *where* it is. The booklet you get from the company, probably titled something like "You and Your Pension—the XYZ Corporation's Retirement Plan," is not the qualified pension plan. The booklet is a *summary plan description*, which, although it may present no conflicts with the qualified pension plan, is not the legal document. Nor is Article XII in your labor contract the qualified pension plan. No matter how detailed a labor contract's pension articles may be, they are only references to the qualified pension plan. (There is one exception—a contract that includes the complete qualified pension plan, usually in an appendix.)

In order to negotiate intelligently, you must have the qualified pension plan itself to study. Since the company may be under the impression that the summary plan description is the controlling document, start early to search for the qualified plan. Otherwise, you may be rousting a bank vice president in the wee hours to recover the document from the company's safe deposit box.

Funding

After both the union and the company have completed negotiations and signed the qualified pension plan, the responsibility for providing the pension benefits rests exclusively with the employer, who has to make sure there is money available to pay the benefits the contract promises. At one time a company was allowed to pay the benefits out of available cash or liquid assets as the benefits came due; now, because of changes in federal law, mainly ERISA, the employer must set aside money on a systematic basis each year to ensure that when a worker is ready to retire, the money will be there to pay the worker's earned benefits. This process of setting aside funds is called *funding* a pension plan.

The Actuary

Needless to say, it's difficult to estimate today how much money should be set aside to pay a benefit 30 or 40 years later. The money will earn interest, but how much? Some people will die before they collect, but how many? In order to determine how much money to set aside each year, the company must hire an *actuary*, an individual trained in the science of making rational or systematic predictions. Like doctors, plumbers, lawyers, and CPAs, actuaries are licensed to practice their trade. Their function in the pension area is to tell employers how much money to set aside each year to provide the money needed to match the benefit obligations. The actuary studies the plan provisions and the age, service, and sex of the employees. He or she then uses that information, estimates turnover, mortality, and fund earnings, and comes up with a "best estimate" of how much should be set aside in order to pay the promised benefit. Because the likelihood of an actuary making accurate predictions in all these areas is slight, *actuarial adjustments* are made periodically (annually in most plans, less frequently in smaller ones) to take care of previous errors. Contribution estimates and supporting figures are then sent to the employer in the form of an *actuarial report*, which tells the company how much to contribute annually in order to fund promised benefits.

The Trustee

The employer turns the money over to a *trustee* who has the responsibility of managing it in the exclusive interests of the individuals covered by the plan. The trustee is usually a bank or commercial insurance carrier. The company signs a trust or contract agreement with this institution that spells out the rights and responsibilities of the two parties (employer and trustee). Once the money passes from employer to trustee, it is no longer the employer's money but belongs to the beneficiaries of the plan. Except in certain limited circumstances (which will be discussed in Chapter 11), the money cannot revert to the company.

When the bank or insurance carrier receives the contribution from the company, the money is invested, either directly or through institutional money managers such as stock and bond specialists. As indicated in Appendix A, the investment options are extensive; in fact, there are still others—the six on the chart are only the most common ones. Each class of investments has certain characteristics of return and risk that make it attractive or unattractive for pension investments, and it is rare to find a pension fund invested solely in one category. Usually a fund would be invested in several categories, as for example 5 percent in cash for liquidity, 75 percent in bonds for security of principal, and 20 percent in stock for growth potential. Whatever the mix, all categories have returns, or earnings, that come back into the trust fund for reinvestment; these are called *fund earnings.*

It should be noted that fund earnings are not necessarily positive. Disregarding income and payouts, the value of a fund at the end of the year can be less than it was in the beginning. This unfortunate situation is called a *negative return on investment,* or *negative earnings.* Fund investments are covered in detail in Chapter 10.

Earnings flow back into the trust for eventual disbursement to participants in the form of monthly or annual pension benefits. Keep in mind that there are two sources, or flows, of money into the trust: employer contributions and fund earnings. The sum of these two flows less administrative expenses should be equal to benefit payments over the long term; that is, until the last participants receive their pensions. The formula for this relationship is

Benefit payments = company contribution + fund earnings − administrative expenses

When this formula holds exactly, there will be just enough money left in the fund to pay the last workers their pensions. It is obvious, however, that given a certain level of benefits and expected payout, the employer's contribution in the short term will depend on assumed fund earnings and, in the long term, on actual fund earnings. The higher the expected and actual fund earnings, the lower the company contribution should be; the lower the expected and actual fund earnings, the higher the company contribution should be. The effect of interest and how to determine a fund's earnings are covered in Chapters 3 and 7.

The Federal Government

National Labor Relations Act

The federal government is involved in nearly every aspect of pensions, not only in making the laws governing labor negotiations and pension management, but in the continued monitoring of labor-management pension agreements.

The legal responsibility of employers to bargain with duly-elected union representatives over wages, hours, and other conditions of employment was established with the passage of the National Labor Relations Act, also known as the Wagner Act, in 1935. It wasn't until 1948, however, that the National Labor Relations Board ruled, in *Inland Steel v. Local 1010, United Steelworkers*, that pension plans are included in "wages, hours, and other conditions of employment." To refuse to bargain over pensions, the NLRB said, was a violation of NLRA Section 8(a)(5). Federal courts subsequently upheld that position.

[*Author's Comment*—The issue of mandatory bargaining over pensions almost never comes up at the table. I say "almost" because in one negotiation a corporate vice president for industrial relations informed me across the table that, while the company was willing to bargain over the normal retirement benefit, the company wasn't about to discuss other aspects of the plan, such as arbitration of pension disputes or the reduction of the normal retirement benefit at early retirement.

I thought the company attorney was going to choke, and before I could get a word out the company had called a recess. The company representatives were back in a few minutes to "clarify" the remarks of the vice president. This time the company attorney did the talking, telling me the company would certainly negotiate on all aspects of the pension plan; the vice president's remarks had been meant only to indicate that the company had more bargaining flexibility in the basic benefit than in other areas of the pension program.

And here I thought the morning was going to provide some comic relief to an otherwise tense and unpleasant negotiation.— J. MacD.]

Although the question of whether pensions are a mandatory bargaining issue is settled, another issue often raised in contract negotiations concerns proposals for pension improvements for people who have already retired.

For example, your bargaining committee reviews the retirement data and finds that people who retired between 1960 and 1969 went out at a benefit formula which called for $3 per month for each year of credited service. The committee quickly realizes that even retirees who had high seniority are now receiving a benefit of less than $100 a month. In light of this, the committee submits a proposal to raise the multiplier from $3 to $6 for this group of retirees. Certainly there would be no lack of arguments justifying this improvement.

Yet occasionally at the bargaining table the company will point out that it is not required to bargain over benefit improvements for individuals who have already retired. In fact, the company may try—improperly—to leave the impression that it is illegal to do this. A quick review of major contract settlements in any given year will show that this is not illegal; many settlements contain pension benefit improvements for retirees. However, it is true that benefit improvements for retirees is not a mandatory bargaining issue. But this does not make a demand for improved pensions for current retirees either illegal or immoral.

The case settling this issue arose shortly after the passage of Medicare in 1965, when the Pittsburgh Plate Glass Company unilaterally modified its retiree health insurance program. The union, Allied Chemical and Alkali Workers of America, filed a claim with the NLRB charging that group health insurance was a mandatory bargaining topic and therefore charged that the company had committed an unfair labor practice by making a unilateral change in the group health program and then refusing to bargain over it. The NLRB held in favor of the union; however, in 1971 the Supreme Court overruled the labor board on the grounds that retired members are not employees under the terms of the NLRA and its amendments. Because the ruling, *Allied Chemical and Alkali Workers v. Pittsburgh Plate Glass Co.*, was based on the NLRA definition of employee, the ruling applies to negotiations on pension improvements as well.

What does this mean in terms of actual negotiations? Very little. The Supreme Court merely said a retiree benefit is not a *mandatory* bargaining item. A retiree benefit is still a permissible, voluntary bargaining item. The only differences are that you can't bargain to impasse or go on strike over a voluntary issue. These two limitations may easily be avoided.

The real distinction between mandatory and permissible issues is bargaining power. If a local union goes into negotiations with little or no economic power (during a recession when half the membership is on layoff, for example), just about everything is voluntary—not in a legal sense but in a practical sense. If the tables are turned and the union is in a strong economic position, the distinction between permissive and mandatory becomes nearly irrelevant when the company is evaluating what it has to do to get a settlement ratified.

[*Author's Comment*—This distinction between permissive and mandatory bargaining was brought home to me dramatically in one auto parts supply negotiation during the recession of the early 1980s. The first meeting with the union's bargaining committee went well in the sense that there was a realistic appraisal of the poor bargaining situation. However, the committee's rather austere initial proposal contained a demand for a substantial increase in retiree pensions.

Legal issues aside, it seemed unrealistic to expect to increase benefits for future retirees, let alone past retirees. When I raised this concern, the committee explained to me that every contract in memory had included something for past retirees. It was a tradition, and the committee couldn't face the membership without some improvement in this area. Being reluctant to trample on tradition, I kept quiet.

It was a tough negotiation, and some long-standing traditions were violated right and left, but when it came to pension improvements for retirees the committee remained adamant: there had to be some improvement. Much to my amazement, the company agreed to improve all past retiree pensions by $.50 per month per year of credited service in the second year of the three-year contract. There was little else to take back to the membership for the ratification vote, but the committee got its past retiree improvement.

Even more enlightening than the company's unexpected movement on this issue was the discussion at the ratification meeting. There was surprisingly little discussion of the two-year wage freeze or the company's demand for modifications in the temporary transfer and seniority provisions. The bulk of the comments centered on the improvement in past retiree pensions. Why was it so small? How come it wasn't effective until the second year? The contract was almost voted down over pension improvements for retirees, the only area where I felt we had a right to be satisfied.

For an attorney to have told this company that bargaining on pensions was voluntary would have been like the robber who holds a gun to your temple and says: "Your money or your life—it's your decision."—J. MacD.]

An associated issue to mandatory bargaining over pensions is the union's right to information about the operation of the plan, a right which derives from the "duty to bargain" section of the NLRA. Chapter 7 includes an extensive discussion of pension documents that should be obtained in order to prepare for bargaining. The NLRB has ruled that "good faith" bargaining includes providing information the union needs to carry out its job effectively. Some companies will question your right to the information, especially the first time you request it. However, you do have a legal right to it and you should push until you have the information you need.

ERISA and the Pension Contract

The federal government's role extends beyond what does or does not happen at the bargaining table. A large body of federal law deals directly and exclusively with pension plans. This body of law has an impact on the whole process.

The major legislation governing present-day pensions is the Employee Retirement Income Security Act of 1974 and its amendments, the most recent of which is the Retirement Equity Act of 1984 (REACT). The major provisions of ERISA, in terms of how they affect the functional relationships of the components of a defined-benefit pension plan, follow below. This is not an exhaustive study, but rather a summary of the highlights.

Before ERISA was passed in 1974, few rules governed the pension contract between union and employer, with the exception that the contract could not discriminate in favor of highly paid personnel such as owners and managers. This was to prevent employers from using pension plans as tax dodges. Other than that, pensions could—and did—vary a great deal. It wasn't unusual to find clauses that made it difficult for the average worker ever to qualify for a pension. Workers could be excluded from participation until age 35, for example, or until a worker had accrued 10 years of service, or until a worker had reached age 35 *and* accrued 10 years of service. Other provisions pushed back vesting until as many as 20 years of service had been accrued.

ERISA established certain minimum standards designed to increase the pension security of workers, so that if you were to study a random selection of contracts today, you would find a core of standards that are very similar in design and effect. Many would be better than the minimum, and none that conform with the law would be worse.

The major standards established cover the following areas.

Participation. Participation standards govern how long a pension contract can delay covering a worker. The original rule was one year or age 25, whichever came later; this was significantly improved in 1984 under REACT to one year or age 21, whichever occurs later.

Vesting. Vesting standards establish a nonforfeitable benefit after a certain number of years of service or age plus service. There are three basic vesting standards: 10-year cliff vesting; graded vesting from 5 to 15 years of service; and vesting by the rule of 45. Vesting provisions are covered at length in Chapter 6.

Definitions of hours and years of service. Without such definitions the two standards above would be meaningless. For example, if a year were not defined, a plan could require 2,080 hours of actual annual work, which would mean that no one who became ill, took a vacation or holiday, or had to take time off for a funeral would ever accumulate a year's service. The definitions are complicated because of industry variations and the ways employers can count time. Hours and service counting methods are discussed in Chapter 6.

Statutory joint and survivor option at retirement. Before ERISA, pension plans either didn't offer spousal benefits or required the participant to specifically select that option. Under ERISA and before REACT, every plan not only had to offer a surviving spouse benefit, but unless the participant specifically rejected the joint and survivor option, his or her spouse was covered automatically. REACT further improved this by making the joint and survivor option automatic unless the spouse as well authorizes the election of a pure or single life annuity. This benefit is covered in detail in Chapter 5.

Preretirement spousal coverage. ERISA established that every plan providing an early retirement option also must provide a preretirement spousal option which would be made available to those who elected not to retire at the early retirement age. This meant, prior to REACT, that the spouse of an individual who elected to work past the early retirement date would be covered under the pension plan if the participant died while actively employed. However, this coverage was at the option of the employee, and the plan was permitted to charge an actuarial reduction for the benefit. This was improved under REACT to apply automatically to vested employees; there may still be an actuarial reduction, however. This coverage is discussed in Chapter 5.

Plan modification and termination. ERISA requires that every contract contain provisions for the modification and termination of a plan, including the crucial determination of how assets will be distributed. This important topic for negotiators is covered in Chapter 11.

Dispute resolution. Each pension plan must contain a dispute resolution procedure. This is of limited value, however, because the appeals procedure from an initial benefit decision doesn't require the dispute to be arbitrated by a neutral third party. Therefore, the person responsible for the initial decision can have a great deal to say about the results of the appeal. This can be remedied by negotiating binding third party arbitration of pension disputes.

Participant information rights. Employee rights were few before ERISA. A worker had, of course, the right of any citizen to use state trust laws or criminal statutes to seek redress against a pension plan. In 1958, the Pension and Welfare Plan Disclosure Act required companies to file information on their pension plans with the Department of Labor. This information, contained on what were then known as D-2 forms, was to be made available to plan participants upon request. With the passage of ERISA, participants' information rights have been considerably expanded. Companies now must provide participants with the following information whether they remember to ask for it or not:

- A summary description of the plan
- A summary of the plan's annual report
- Any material modifications or amendments which occurred during the plan year

Further, anyone whose employment terminates during the year must receive a statement of vested benefits.

The company is obligated to give participants the following information only upon request:

- A statement of accrued and vested benefits once a year
- A copy of the full plan document
- The latest annual report
- The trust agreement or insurance contract

The company may charge a participant a reasonable fee for any of this optional information.

ERISA did not establish any new rights and responsibilities for labor organizations, although it has had an indirect effect on unions' behavior by creating contractual minimums and providing direct information to union members. However, the plan administrator (usually the company) is considerably affected by ERISA. The law requires the plan administrator to

- Provide the participant with a summary plan description;
- Provide the summary annual report; and
- File a form known as a DOL 5500, including an actuarial report, with the Department of Labor.

In terms of contributions, ERISA changes the company's liability considerably. Before ERISA, the focus of the law was on preventing a company from using a pension trust for tax-reduction purposes; thus the law was written in terms of the yearly maximum a company could contribute. The employer's minimum contribution had to cover benefits accrued during that year, plus interest on any unfunded liability. Under ERISA, companies have to make contributions toward any unfunded liability over and above the interest. For past service unfunded liability outstanding on January 1, 1974, the period for write-off was 40 years for liability. For unfunded liability incurred in 1974 or after, resulting from plan amendments or adoption of a new plan, the write-off period is 30 years.

Pension Benefit Guaranty Corporation

One of the biggest problems associated with the private pension system before ERISA was the reduction of accrued benefits, which often occurred during plan terminations involving plant closings. Because of long-term funding of benefits, there were frequently insufficient assets to pay all accrued benefits. To remedy this, at least partially, ERISA provided for the establishment of the *Pension Benefit Guaranty Corporation (PBGC)*, a federally sponsored insurance company that guarantees a percentage of accrued pension benefits. This part of ERISA is more fully explored in Chapter 11, which deals with plant closings.

There are other ramifications of ERISA, but these are the main ones that will affect you in negotiations. The relationships between union, company, trustee, and government are complicated and interconnected, but should become clearer as the book progresses.

3

How a Pension Works

Today's rapidly changing economic and legal climate has put the private pension system under considerable stress. The result has been that companies are looking for alternate methods of providing retirement income, methods which are called "pensions" but which differ considerably in philosophy and design from the typical negotiated plan. Therefore, it is important that you, as a pension negotiator, clearly understand what a pension plan is, what the nature of the retirement income promise is, and how money is accumulated to meet that promise.

This chapter introduces the basic features of the typical negotiated pension plan, gives you a bench mark for critically evaluating different approaches to providing retirement income, and provides some tools that will be helpful both later in the book and in actual negotiations. You'll also have a chance to look over the shoulders of the union at Mythical Plating Company, Local 3520, as the committee develops a basic retirement plan to propose during the upcoming contract negotiations.

What a Pension Is

The typical negotiated pension plan may be defined as *a group savings plan that has the exclusive purpose of providing a secure retirement income for those who leave the work force because of age*. While this definition isn't perfect, it does highlight key features of the negotiated pension.

A Group Plan

A pension is a plan that provides benefits on a *group* basis rather than an individual basis. This approach has both advantages and disadvantages. A key advantage is that it is less costly to provide pension benefits on a group basis (the reason will become clear in a few pages); so a plan can provide greater retirement benefits for the same cost.

A disadvantage is that because a pension is a group plan, some people won't be paid benefits even though they may have worked for several years as participants in the plan. This is because most negotiated pension plans require participants to work for a company for a considerable length of time, most commonly 10 years, before they are vested. Anyone who leaves before he or she is vested usually forfeits all rights to pension benefits at normal retirement age.

This group nature of the plan will be a major concern of the pension contract language you'll be negotiating. You'll have to decide, for example, how someone becomes eligible for a pension and when he or she can leave employment and still be eligible for benefits. As will become clear when Local 3520 begins to wrestle with setting up its pension, some difficult choices face the union negotiator. Every time the group of potential beneficiaries is expanded through improved contract language in negotiations, it costs the company (or the company and the participants) more money. Negotiators frequently are faced with a choice: improve the benefits for the current group, or keep benefits the same and expand eligibility to more members. It is not an easy choice.

A Savings Plan

A pension is first and foremost a group *savings* plan. The decision to begin a pension program, or to improve an existing one, means that a group of workers has decided to defer some current benefit in favor of a future benefit—retirement income.

From a collective bargaining standpoint the philosophical aspects of a pension are less important than the practical aspect of a pension as a savings plan. If local union leaders want a good retirement plan, they need to make the pension fund a priority at contract time. This won't always be easy or popular; better wages, more holidays, and improved vacations are often of more immediate concern to your membership. The committee at Mythical Plating will run into the "get the money now" argument from several members of the local, such as Sam G., who runs out of cash every week a couple of days before payday, and Bess E., who has perfected the art of "forgetting" to sign the checks she pays her heating bill with.

And what if the whole operation is moved to Mexico, or sold to Bigwerks, the plating operation across town? The concerns of day-to-day living will always be more real to the membership than providing for a shadowy future 30 years away. When a strong pension program exists, it is almost always because the local union has had strong, responsible leaders who see the value of a pension and who build a consensus among the membership to support plan improvements. Good pensions take time to build, because the leadership has to educate not only the company but its own membership.

Local union leaders also have to make certain that members will get a good deal 30 years from now for the wages and fringes they forgo today. While there may not be an exact, penny-for-penny relationship in a particular negotiation between a wage increase forgone and the hourly cost of a pension improvement gained, there is obviously *some* relationship. However, as you will see, the cost of a pension plan can vary significantly from year to year.

[*Author's Comment*—In one negotiation I was involved with, the company made a lot of noise about the "high cost" of the local union's proposed pension improvements. The company dragged in all sorts of diagrams and charts to illustrate its point. In the final hours of negotiations, the committee, very concerned with pension improvement, accepted the company's position that "you can take x cents in additional wage improvements or you can take that same money and increase the monthly pension benefits so many dollars a month per year of service."

Three years later, during the next round of negotiations, the committee and I decided to track the company's pension contributions. We found that, while the benefit in the first year of the contract had indeed been funded at the level the company promised ($.53 an hour, a $.10 an hour increase over the final year under the former contract), in the second year the benefit was funded at $.40 an hour and in the third, at $.35 an hour.

This meant that while members had given up $.10 an hour in wages for the pension improvement, in the final year of the contract the company was getting by for $.08 an hour less than the $.43 they had been paying before the contract was negotiated. The workers had sacrificed $.10 an hour in wages to buy future benefits which had cost the company nothing.

It was a good deal for the company, but not for the workers. This underscores the importance of not only reviewing pension benefits before each contract negotiation, but also of making sure that any current benefits sacrificed are in fact going to provide improved benefits for your members' retirement rather than for the company's present balance sheet.—J. MacD.]

A Retirement Income Plan

The third important element of a pension is its exclusive concentration on providing *retirement income*. While this might seem obvious, it is not unusual to find pension plans loaded with extras. These include death benefits, which look remarkably like life insurance, as well as cash-out provisions which allow participants access to their accrued benefits for immediate cash. At first glance these features appear desirable, but loading a pension with obligations to do anything but provide retirement income reduces the program's likelihood of actually providing that income.

Therefore, whether you are designing a pension from scratch or modifying an existing program, ask yourself if each proposal is going to improve the amount and security of retirement income. If the proposal is really an attempt to solve another problem through the pension mechanism, try to find another approach to solving the problem, one that doesn't involve the pension. Look into alternatives such as improving life insurance benefits, starting a credit union or payroll savings plan, negotiating supplemental unemployment benefits, or adding long-term disability insurance.

A Dependable Income

The fourth important aspect of a pension is *security*. The whole point of setting up a pension plan is to provide a retired person with a dependable source of income that, combined with Social Security, will ensure a comfortable standard of living. This focus on pension security has implications for how the plan is structured and for the scope of the negotiator's responsibilities to the membership.

Most negotiated plans provide a specific retirement income benefit rather than a contribution rate (for example, a benefit of $10 per month per year of service rather than a contribution of $.85 per hour worked). This structure is no accident. It comes from the belief that an essential element of security is the ability to predict exactly how much retirement income you are entitled to. You can only do this if the actual benefit is spelled out in the contract, as in a defined-benefit plan. Most union pensions are structured this way.

Because the focus of the negotiator is on the benefit rather than the contribution, it is easy to forget about the pension once the collective bargaining agreement has been signed. But if you are truly concerned about pension security, you'll have to remain involved. You must be sure enough money Is being set aside to provide the benefits, and that this money is being invested prudently. ERISA went a long way in dealing with this security issue, but if your plant closes, it is still possible that your members will be confronted with sizable reductions in pension benefits they were depending on. It is the negotiator's responsibility, through the contract, to minimize the likelihood of this happening.

How Pensions Differ from Other Savings Plans

These key ideas—the group nature of pensions, deferred income (savings), retirement income as the exclusive goal, and security—form the basis of the pension discussions in this book. Once you understand these principles you'll be on your way to becoming a competent negotiator in the pension area.

With these elements in mind, the bargaining committee of Local 3520 has decided to set up a simplified pension plan at Mythical Plating. It is due to have its first meeting a week from Thursday; in the meantime, Fred Washington, one of the committee members, has started fiddling with his calculator to produce some numbers to present at the meeting.

Income Goals

Fred decides to set up a hypothetical pension plan for himself, to see how it will work for the rest of the membership. His first thought concerns how much he can afford to set aside each year for retirement. Not knowing where to begin, he picks some random figures and comes up with the following:

As a first effort, he finds saving $2 a year is ridiculously low. At the end of 30 years, he'll have a grand total of $60, plus interest, on which to live out his life.

Next he tries $50 a year. That would give him $1,500 plus interest; assuming he retired at 65 and died at 66, he and his wife would have enough to live on for one year.

Fred tries another number. This time he goes for broke and figures out what his retirement income would be if he put aside

$4,500 a year: a nest egg of $135,000 plus a good amount of interest that he doesn't calculate at this point in his thinking. He and his wife could live fairly well on that for a while, assuming the house is paid for and the winters are mild. But trying to save $4,500 every year for 30 years, on his wages, would certainly make the years between now and then difficult.

Fred has just discovered a basic problem of pension planning: how to provide adequate retirement income while minimizing his present sacrifices.

He tries a few more numbers, with mixed success, before it occurs to him that it makes more sense to work backwards and decide how much he wants to have coming in each month when he retires. For the sake of argument, he decides on an income of $100 a month, and also, for purposes of this exercise, that he'll retire at age 65, when he is eligible for full Social Security benefits.

Participant's Life Expectancy

No sooner has Fred solved one problem than he runs right into another. He knows he wants $100 a month ($1,200 a year) but how much will he need at age 65 to provide for the rest of his life? Obviously, this is $1,200 multiplied by how long he is going to live, but just how will he figure out how long he'll live after he retires? He read somewhere that the life expectancy of the average American is about 72 years, but if he uses that figure in his calculations, chances are the money will run out long before both he and his wife have died. That is because age 72 is an average life expectancy for the whole population, including infants who die soon after being born. The curious thing about life expectancy is that the longer you live, the longer you are likely to live. At age 2, for example, the probability of reaching age 90 is relatively small. However, if you're 89, the odds of reaching 90 are very much improved. Applied to pension income, this means that people who reach age 65 are a fairly healthy lot, and on the average they will live until age 80, a full 15 years after retirement. Because women live five years longer than men, on the average, his wife can expect to live until she's 85; since she is five years older than Fred, she has as many years left as he does.

Fred thinks he has the problem solved. If he multiplies $1,200 by the 15 years he expects to live after retirement, he'd have to save $18,000 over the next 30 years, or about $600 per year.

Effect of Interest on the Needed Lump Sum

But on the way home Fred passes the bank, which has a sign out front advertising passbook savings accounts that pay 6 percent interest. Interest! He hadn't taken into account that every deposit he makes will earn interest to enable him to reduce the yearly contribution.

Fred doesn't have time to stop at the bank to check out his theory, but he's right. At the end of 30 years at 6 percent interest, the actual amount in his bank account at a savings rate of $600 per year would be $47,434.92, not $18,000.

Further, when he starts withdrawing his $100 a month, the entire remaining amount is going to continue to grow because of the interest. The upshot is that if Fred and his wife live only 15 years after his retirement, as is his expectation, there will be a lot of cash left over, something the couple would rather avoid. They will have saved more than they had to. Philosophical discussions of the value of thrift to the contrary, on Fred's income there isn't room for extra savings.

As you can see, interest complicates pension planning. Next evening, Fred tries to figure out how to avoid saving too much for retirement. Finally, he decides he needs professional help and calls the county library. The librarian suggests he stop by after work tomorrow to look at the interest rate tables.

The next day, after thumbing through several pages of tables, Fred comes across one called *Present Value of $1 Received Annually for N Years* (Appendix B). By consulting this table, Fred will learn how much money to deposit today so that it will pay him $1 a year for a given number of years, taking into account the interest earnings on the money left in the fund.

In Fred's case, he wants the payout to be $1,200 a year for 15 years ($18,000 total), so he reads down the 6 percent column until he reaches 15 years and finds the amount: $9.712. This tells him he would need to have saved a total of $9.712 to pay out $1 a year for 15 years after retirement; to figure his desired retirement income of $1,200 a year, he multiplies $9.712 × $1,200 = $11,654.40.

For another approach, note that if it takes $9.712 to generate $1 a year for 15 years, interest earnings will provide $5.29 of that $15 total ($15 − $9.712 = $5.29), roughly 35 percent of the required total. If Fred and his wife want to receive $18,000 during retirement, they can count on 6 percent interest generating about

35 percent of that amount. That's about $6,346 in interest; subtracting the interest from the total amount they need gives them the total they need to save: $11,653.20 (The total differs slightly from the one in the previous example because of rounding.)

Thus, if they save $11,654.40 by the time he retires, and if everything else goes as expected (neither lives longer than 15 years after retirement, and the interest rate doesn't decline), they should be able to pay themselves $100 a month for exactly 15 years, and not have any money left over.

Now Fred has a goal: $11,654.40 by the time he reaches age 65. He figures if he divides it into 30 equal deposits he will have to save only $388 a year to reach that goal. But he's not out of the woods yet; the interest factor continues to complicate things. Saving $388 a year would mean Fred still would end up with nearly three times the amount he needs. Although this would triple his retirement income, his preference now is to defer as little as possible from current wages.

Fred needs to return to the interest tables to consult one called *Future Values of an Annuity of $1* (Appendix C). This table tells him the eventual size (after N amount of years) of an interest-bearing fund into which $1 is put each year. Fred's savings fund is going to be around for the next 30 years, so he reads down the Years (N) column to 30 and across to the column marked with the interest he expects to earn—6 percent. This figure, rounded to the third decimal, is $79.058. It means that if Fred puts aside a dollar each year, and earns a consistent 6 percent interest rate on that money, those dollars will grow to $79.058 after 30 years. To convert that example into the amount he needs to save each year for the total, including interest, to be the $11,654.40 he needs at retirement, Fred divides the amount he wants ($11,654.40) by the amount generated at age 65 by putting $1 aside each year at 6 percent ($79.058).

$$\$11,654.40 \div \$79.058 = \$147.42$$

The result is a yearly contribution of $147.42, roughly one-third of the $388 he would need to contribute each year if he didn't take interest into account.

(It is interesting to contemplate what Fred would have had to save if interest were not available: $18,000 rather than $11,654.40, and $600 a year rather than $147.42. The payout is $18,000 either way, but without interest he would be saving $18,000 to receive $18,000. With interest, he pays only $4,422.60 ($147.42 × 30) to get an $18,000 return—a 75 percent savings.)

And that's how Fred put together a pension plan for himself and his wife. Although it took a lot of time and research, his retirement income is not truly secure, because he had to make several major assumptions, including how much he'll need to live on 30 years from now, how long he'll live, and what interest rate his money will be earning all that time.

How Age Affects Cost

Of course, the results of Fred's calculations would be different were he younger or older, or if he were to assume a different rate of return on the earnings before and after age 65. A table showing *The Effect of Age on Pension Cost* (Appendix D) demonstrates the difference. A simple inspection of this table will show you a couple of important things.

First, the older the individual is, the more a $100 per month retirement program costs. Each year's contribution must be larger because there are both fewer years in which to accumulate the money and fewer years in which the interest can accumulate. As you can see in the 6 percent column, starting a retirement fund at age 60 will cost $2,067.45 a year to save enough for a $100 a month payment; interest earnings provide only 10 percent of the needed sum. On the other hand, if you start a retirement fund at age 20, you need to put away only $54.68 a year, because interest will account for 79 percent of the necessary amount. The difference is so dramatic because each year interest accumulates on the interest earned in previous years. In time the compounded interest surpasses the contributions made to the principal each year.

How Interest Rates Affect Cost

Second, the table indicates that at any given age, the required contribution falls dramatically with a relatively small increase in interest earnings. For example, if Fred had assumed an 8 percent rate rather than 6 percent, his yearly contribution would have dropped from $147.42 to $90.66, a 38 percent drop in costs.

Looking at it another way, if he had contributed $147.42 at 8 percent, in 30 years he would have generated $16,700.20 rather than $11,654.40. Translated to a monthly income, he would have an income of $162.60, roughly a 60 percent increase in benefits from a 2 percent increase in the interest rate.

After all the time Fred has put into his do-it-yourself retirement fund, he's feeling pretty confident about the pension meeting next week. He has learned a thing or two about setting income goals and interest-contribution relationships. He wonders if there's anything left to worry about—can't the committee just take his plan and multiply the annual contribution by the number of the people in the bargaining unit?

The Group Aspect of Pensions

When Local 3520 was organized three years ago, the committee talked about a pension plan but other issues were more important at the time, such as the average wage. The committee made progress on wages in the first contract, so now it is more comfortable about seeking a retirement program. As a result of Fred's calculations, the committee has decided to shoot for $100 per month for a member retiring at age 65.

When the committee members meet Thursday evening at the union office, the first thing they do is look over a printout the financial secretary obtained from the company personnel manager. The printout lists all members of the bargaining unit by name, date of hire, and date of birth. Leroy Smith, the bargaining committee chair, has gone a step further and organized on a yellow legal pad the number of members who are each age. By coincidence, all 41 members have ages ending in 0 or 5, so it is a relatively brief list.

Age 60	2 members	Age 40	4 members
Age 55	5 members	Age 35	0 members
Age 50	0 members	Age 30	20 members
Age 45	10 members	Ages 25 and 20	0 members

As you can see, the membership ranges in age from 60 to 30. It seems logical to use Fred's procedure to estimate how much to set aside to provide $100 a month for each of the 41 members, by determining an annual contribution for each person and then totaling the individual contribution figures. In fact, while the rest of the committee gets sidetracked in chitchat, Fred goes to work on Leroy's list. To take care of the two 60-year-olds, for example, would require $2,067.45 each at 6 percent, or $4,134.90 for the pair. Fred writes that figure down, and goes through a similar calculation for the 30-year-olds, whose individual requirements are $104.37 each.

The annual contribution needed for all 20 of the 30-year-olds would be 20 × $104.37, or $2,087.40 a year.

Following that procedure for the rest of the bargaining unit, Fred determines that it would be necessary to set aside $14,659.26 a year for the pension fund, which works out to $357.54 per member ($14,659.26 ÷ 41 members = $357.54). In cents-per-hour (the standard way of referring to costs during negotiations), the set-aside would be $.18 an hour for a 2,000 hour year ($357.63 ÷ 2000 = $.1788, roughly $.18 an hour).

Here's what his calculations look like:

Age	Number of Members	Annual Contribution per Individual	Annual Contribution per Age Group
60	2	$2,067.45	$ 4,134.90
55	5	884.20	4,421.00
50	0	—	—
45	10	316.82	3,168.20
40	4	211.94	847.76
35	0	—	—
30	20	104.37	2,087.40
25	0	—	—
20	0	—	—
	41		$14,659.26

If determining the funding needed were only that simple, the bargaining committee could adjourn right now. But there's a catch.

Effects of Turnover and Mortality

The goal is to provide an adequate retirement income for *the least possible cost*. If the committee stops now, and somehow convinces the company to set aside $.18 an hour per worker, the company will be deferring entirely too much money, money that would be better spent on other contract improvements, such as the average wage.

Why would the plan be overfunded at $.18 an hour? Well, one of the 30-year-olds is talking about going back to school to become an industrial hygienist. He'll probably quit his job at the beginning of the fall semester. Roy M. smokes too much, drinks too much, and drives too fast, and even he isn't betting he'll see his 65th birthday. Other members will move out of town, get better jobs someplace else, or just quit. The upshot is that, for one reason or another, a number of the employees now at Mythical won't be around to collect their $100 a month retirement income.

If some people are not going to collect, the committee need not plan to have money put aside for them. Its problem is figuring who those people will be.

Actuarial Assumptions and Cost

Fortunately, actuaries make their living predicting how many people are going to die or otherwise terminate employment at certain ages. They make these predictions, called *actuarial assumptions*, by observing large groups of people and tallying the results in the form of *mortality tables* (see Appendix E) and *turnover tables*.

These tables are quite accurate for large groups of people, although the experience of Local 3520, with only 41 members, probably will differ slightly from the tables' predictions. For example, one learns from the table in Appendix E that 91.2 percent of the 60-year-olds will reach age 65; for Local 3520, that means that only 1.82 of the two 60-year-olds will be alive in five years, not a likely outcome. But there is no reason to believe the general experience of Local 3520 will vary significantly from the large-group experience reflected in the mortality and turnover tables.

The cost effects of mortality and turnover are calculated in much the same way. When you look at the mortality table in Appendix E you will see that the first column lists age; the second column lists those alive at a given age out of an initial group of one million, and the third column gives the percentage of those in the first column who will live to age 65. For example, if you run down the first column to age 40, and over to the third column, you will find the figure 79.3. This means that nearly 80 percent of those alive at age 40 (793,521 of the initial one million people) will live to age 65. (The slight difference is due to rounding off, which is necessary when dealing with numbers in a table.)

Therefore, if you have 100 40-year-olds in the shop, you have to set aside money for only 79.3 of them. Local 3520 has four 40-year-olds, with a total annual contribution of $847.76 needed for the four of them; because only 79.3 percent will actually collect, the committee needs to set aside only $672.27 ($847.76 × .793 − $672.27).

When the local adjusts each age group for mortality, the figures will look like the ones in Columns 4, 5, and 6 of *Pension Costs Adjusted for Mortality and Turnover* (Appendix F). The total annual contribution needed, taking mortality into consideration, is $12,406.17, some $2,250 less than the initial calculation of $14,659.26, a savings of over 15 percent. The reduction in contribution because of job turnover (see Column 7) would be calculated the same way, although turnover tables are somewhat less accurate than mortality tables because of the individual nature of a job quit. The cost-reducing effects of mortality and turnover are calculated in Column 8 of Appendix F. With both discounts taken into consideration, the annual contribution Local 3520 needs to extract from the company drops to $12,081.92, an 18 percent savings. Translated into a cents-per-hour cost, divide first by the number of members and then by the average annual hours worked:

$$\$12,081.92 \div 41 = \$294.68 \div 2,000 = \$.147$$

This 15 cents an hour cost is a reduction of 3 cents an hour because of mortality and turnover, money that can be used for insurance, hourly wage increases, paid holidays, or other benefits.

Summary

It is obvious that the deliberations of Local 3520 have been simplified. Few negotiated plans call for a flat dollar amount at retirement regardless of service. But benefit formula aside, the principle in all negotiated defined-benefit plans is the same. The contract contains a specific promise of retirement income rather than a commitment about the size of the company contribution. This approach is designed to improve pension security and predictability.

No legal pension plan in existence today limits retirement benefits only to those who reach age 65. However, because of the group nature of negotiated pension plans, there will always be the issue of who is in and who is not in the group. This will be one of the major issues the bargaining committee of Local 3520 will have to deal with as it refines and improves the pension program. It is easy to see that, unfortunately, broadening the scope of the group to include quits or the families of deceased members will cost money.

Remember, too, that because Local 3520's plan is so simple, the rough-cost estimates are straightforward. As retirement formulas and eligibility rules become more complex, so will cost-estimate problems. However, the principle of systematically setting aside money based on certain assumptions regarding future interest, mortality, turnover, and income need never changes; it is applicable to any pension plan.

Finally, regardless of how simple or complex the plan, the estimates are still nothing more than guesses that are subject to annual revision While from a practical standpoint it is often fruitless to argue about these guesses, it is important to look for any changes in the assumptions that may allow you to negotiate benefit increases at no cost to the company or the membership.

In the next chapter you will use these basic principles of the typical negotiated plan to evaluate its major competitor in providing retirement income: the defined-contribution pension plan.

4

Defined-Benefit and Defined-Contribution Plans

In the previous chapter, the pension plan set up by Local 3520 centered around a specific benefit: $100 a month for each retiree. If the local succeeds in its bargaining goal, the company will set aside money on a systematic basis so funds will be readily available to meet the pension obligation. This type of arrangement is called a defined-benefit pension plan.

However, Local 3520 could have set up its pension as a defined-contribution plan, which is very different both in philosophy and structure. This chapter will examine the advantages and disadvantages of each.

What the Benefit Is

While a defined-benefit plan contains a specific promise of how much a retired member will receive each month or each year, there is no such promise in a defined-contribution plan. A defined-contribution pension specifies only the amount to be contributed to the plan. The retirement benefit is the amount contributed plus whatever earnings accrue to the contributions during the participant's employment less administrative expenses. Since no one can predict with certainty what earnings might be over the next 30 years, it is all but impossible to estimate what retirement benefit to expect under such a plan.

For example, if you negotiate a defined-contribution plan that calls for a contribution of $.50 per hour worked (roughly $1,000 a year, assuming a 2,000-hour year), the benefit accumulated by a

34

worker who is 35 now and who will be working continuously until retirement at age 65 could vary by more than 500 percent, depending on what that $.50 per hour contribution has been able to earn. Here's how the situation looks, at various interest rates, after 30 years, translated first into annual and monthly annuity rates, and then into comparable defined-benefit accrual rates.

Table 4–1. Effect of Interest on a $.50 per Hour Defined-Contribution Pension Plan

Interest on Account	0%	2%	4%	6%	8%	10%
Account value after 30 years	$30,000	$40,568	$56,084	$79,058	$113,238	$164,494
Annual annuity income from lump sum at age 65	$2,000	$3,157	$5,044	$8,140	$13,230	$21,627
Monthly annuity income (annual annuity ÷ 12)	$166.67	$263.08	$420.33	$678.33	$1,102.50	$1,802.25
Comparable defined-benefit accrual rate (monthly annuity ÷ years of service)*	$5.56	$8.77	$14.01	$22.61	$36.75	$60.08

*Dollar amount per month per year of service

The difference between the two kinds of plans is between a predictable benefit with a variable contribution (defined-benefit plan) and a predictable contribution with a variable benefit (defined-contribution plan). This difference is very important, because an essential element of retirement security is the knowledge that a certain level of benefit will be waiting for you. With a defined-contribution plan, you don't know how much you can count on until you're ready to retire.

How Age Affects the Benefit

Another important difference emerges when you compare the retirement benefits accrued by two workers at the same plant, one age 35 and one age 55, under a defined-contribution plan that has just gone into effect. Assuming a $.50 per hour contribution and steady earnings of 6 percent, when both workers retire the 35-year-old will have $79,058 accrued, while the 55-year-old will have been able to accrue only $13,180. Translated into a monthly benefit, this means the 55-year-old will have a pension of $118.30 to look forward to, while the 35-year-old will get a monthly check for $678.49 at retirement. The calculations look like this:

Table 4–2. Effect of Age on Benefit Accrual
(Assuming a $.50 per Hour Defined-Contribution Pension Plan)

Age	Accrued at 65	Principal	Interest	Annual Benefit	Monthly Benefit	Comparable Defined-Benefit Accrual Rate
55	$13,180	$10,000	$ 3,180	$1,539.71	$128.30	$12.83/month/year
35	$79,058	$30,000	$49,058	$8,141.88	$678.49	$19.38/month/year

The inequities of the yearly accrual rates are obvious, even taking into account the effect of inflation over the next 30 years. The younger worker accrues more than $6 per month per year over the older worker. The important thing for a negotiator to remember is that the difference is due to the effect of age on accrual rates. Later in this chapter you'll learn how to compensate for this.

Individual Versus Group Funding

Another important difference between defined-benefit and defined-contribution plans is the existence in the latter of individual accounts (although defined contribution plans may involve a trust fund into which contributions are pooled and from which benefits determined by the trustees are paid). The typical negotiated plan is a group plan promising benefits not to individuals but to the group. Therefore, a worker participating in a defined-benefit plan does not have an account in his or her name specifying how much money is set aside to pay his or her retirement benefit; instead, a pool of assets is set aside to satisfy the expected liabilities of the group. This concept is not always understood, particularly at contract ratification meetings, where someone always wants to know "what the company did with Joe's pension money," Joe being anyone who terminated employment by quitting, dying, becoming disabled, and so on, before becoming vested.

As you recall from the previous chapter, "Joe" never had a specific amount put aside on his behalf; the local knew from the mortality and turnover tables that not all of the people in the original bargaining unit would be around to collect the pension. That assumption is built into the contribution necessary for a defined-benefit plan, and allows higher benefits for those who retire after satisfying eligibility requirements (not that this makes it any easier to explain things to a worker who gets fired a few months before becoming vested).

Defined-contribution plans, on the other hand, usually *do* have individual accounts. Any employee can go to the plan administrator's office and see the value of his or her account on any specific day because the money is earmarked for each individual. This aspect of defined-contribution plans, called *individual funding*, has several pros and cons in terms of retirement income security.

Advantages of Individual Funding

The following are some advantages to individual funding.

Simplicity. Because defined-contribution plans are individual accounts, much of the complexity of a pension plan is eliminated, such as defining who is eligible to receive benefits. Most of the vesting rules, determination of hours, and early retirement reductions that characterize defined-benefit plans are irrelevant to a defined-contribution plan.

Immediate vesting. Most defined-benefit plans contain lengthy requirements for vesting, typically 10 years. Defined-contribution plans typically provide for immediate or close-to-immediate vesting.

100 percent funding. Because there is no benefit amount specified in a defined-contribution plan, it is by definition always fully funded. A participant's plan balance is what the participant will receive.

Portability. Because the accounts are individual ones, and because most defined-contribution plans allow cash-outs upon termination, workers can take their accumulated income with them when they change jobs. If there's a defined-contribution plan at the new work location it's a simple matter to deposit the money from the old plan into the new one. If an employer-sponsored plan does not exist, it is easy to roll over the cash-out into an individual retirement account (IRA). This portability rarely exists with a defined-benefit plan, unless the plan is a multiemployer plan and the individual switches jobs from one participating employer to another.

Disadvantages of Individual Funding

Disadvantages of individual funding include the following.

Expense. Because all participants receive a benefit, there is no cost discount accruing from workers who never become vested, as in a defined-benefit plan. While this appears equitable, it makes it more expensive—hence harder—to obtain an adequate retirement income for your members.

The balance between individual equity and costs associated with providing improved vesting and survivorship is constantly changing. At one time it was not unusual to find 20-year vesting requirements and extremely limited survivor benefits. Today, 10-year vesting is coming under increased attack as too long, and unions are negotiating much-improved survivor benefits. While these changes increase the cost of providing retirement income, it can be argued that they improve the individual equity of a defined-benefit plan.

[*Author's comment*—One plan I'm familiar with allowed participants to draw on their accounts if they were laid off for more than a week.

As it happened, each summer the plant had a two-week June shutdown. I asked one of the bargaining committee members, who looked about 50 years old, how much he had in his individual account after 10 years. You guessed it: his account was empty. Each summer he had used his account balance to fund his vacation.

Of course, he solemnly informed me he was concerned about retirement and intended to stop this practice very soon. I didn't have the heart to tell him that it was already too late. The adequacy of retirement income in a defined-contribution plan depends heavily on the interest earnings on accumulated contributions and, even more importantly, on the compounding effects of interest on interest. The compounding effect becomes significant only after extended periods of time. With only 10 to 15 years left before retirement, this committee member didn't have enough time for the dramatic effects of compounding to occur.—J. MacD.]

Who bears the risk. Regardless of whether a pension is a defined-contribution or a defined-benefit plan, its assets are invested in various financial instruments ranging from Treasury bills to high-risk common stock. All instruments carry some degree of risk, and someone or some institution has to face that risk. In a defined-benefit plan, it is the plan itself (or the plan sponsor, in most cases the employer) who bears the risk. For example, at one time it was not uncommon for pension funds to earn a negative rate of return because the assets were worth less at the end of the year than they were at the beginning. This had no impact on the benefit promises contained in defined-benefit plans. If a plan promised $10 a month per year of credited service, that's what people got, regardless of what was happening in the financial market. If bad investments meant the plan had asset deficiencies, it was the plan's responsibility to make good on those losses (the exception would be in a plan termination, which is discussed in Chapter 11).

The defined-contribution plan is just the opposite. The plan or plan sponsor faces no market risk at all. The participant is the one who faces the risk associated with a certain set of investments.

For example, a local union has a defined-contribution plan with the assets invested in an indexed account (which means the investments are keyed to the stock market). Jody has participated in the plan for 30 years; she's now 64, and intends to retire next year when she's eligible for full Social Security. This year her account balance is $50,000; if she could go to a commercial insurance carrier now, she could get a monthly retirement benefit of $500. But next year, her retirement year, is going to be a bad year for the market. The indexed fund will fall by 25 percent, and so will her account, down $12,500 to $37,500. That will leave her with only enough to buy an annuity yielding $375 a month, rather than the $500 a month she could have purchased had she retired before the index fell. Although investment managers always say that the stock market will beat inflation in the long run, that's no help to Jody, who wants to retire in the short run and has to absorb a 25 percent reduction in pension benefits in the process.

Negligible credit for past service. When a defined-benefit plan is established or improved, union negotiators often are able to arrange credit for past service. This means that someone who is close to retirement when the pension plan or improvement goes into effect receives full or partial credit for years worked. Defined-contribution plans don't cover past service because there is no benefit promised. The difference in the two benefits can be substantial.

Consider what could happen to Rex, for example, who is a month shy of his 65th birthday with 30 years' seniority. In one scenario, he's covered by a defined-benefit pension that entitles him to a retirement benefit equal to $10 a month per year of credited service. In another scenario, he is a participant in a defined-contribution plan with an account balance of roughly $30,000. So far, there is no difference. But, this week the union is negotiating a new contract, and Rex is uppermost in the committee's minds. They want to do the best they can for him.

If they're negotiating the first scenario, they may be able to get a $1 to $2 increase in benefits over the life of the contract. For someone with 30 years of service, this would mean an increase of $30 to $60 a month in the retirement benefit—not enough to change someone's lifestyle, but sufficient to give Rex some pocket change.

Negotiating the same increase under the second scenario would be impossible. A $30-per-month-for-life annuity has a value of about $3,000. Rex has only 180 hours left to work before he reaches 65; therefore, the committee would have to negotiate an hourly contribution of $16.67 ($3,000 ÷ 180 = $16.67). If negotiating a $16 per hour contribution isn't impossible, nothing is.

Disability. The typical defined-contribution plan provides for the right of the worker to liquidate the account in the event of disability. However, an individual rarely becomes disabled according to the seniority roster. Factory work, for example, involves heavy labor; some industrial workers become disabled after relatively short periods of employment. These individuals' defined-contribution accounts will be small, certainly too small to provide an income for the rest of their lives. This is also true for relatively long-service employees. A defined-benefit pension is much more adaptable, and most provide for a lifetime disability benefit after a period of service that typically is set at 10 years.

Table 4–3 summarizes how the two types of plan differ.

Hybrid Plans

Under ERISA it is the nature of the promises contained in the qualified pension plan, not those in the labor agreement, that

---

Table 4–3. Summary of Major Differences Between Defined-Benefit and Defined-Contribution Plans

Defined-Benefit	Defined-Contribution
Promised benefit; benefit can be calculated	Promised contribution; benefit can only be estimated
Group provision of benefits	Individual accounts
Fund bears market risk	Individual bears risk
Lengthy vesting requirements	Immediate or almost-immediate vesting
Favors older worker	Favors younger worker
Can accomplish a great deal at bargaining table for those about to retire	Cannot accomplish much at bargaining table for those about to retire
Substantial credit for past service	No credit for past service
Potential for good disability coverage	Poor disability coverage

---

determine whether a pension is a defined-contribution or a defined-benefit plan. Some plans appear to have features of both defined-benefit and defined-contribution plans. These hybrids occur most often in multiemployer plans because they are the only practical way to fund a master plan with large numbers of participating employers. However, similar arrangements exist occasionally in single-employer plans for reasons that are mainly historical. In order to get a pension started, a union would negotiate a certain cents-per-hour contribution at the bargaining table and subsequently design a defined-benefit pension around the cents-per-hour contribution, continuing the approach in future negotiations. However, these plans are still considered defined-benefit plans under the law.

How to Offset the Disadvantages of Defined-Contribution Plans

Although a defined-contribution plan has a number of positive features, such as immediate vesting and 100 percent funding, most unions have, and prefer to keep, defined-benefit plans. The major reason for this is benefit security. In the case of a defined-contribution plan, the potential for liquidating individual accounts during layoff or other job separation, the dependence on long-term returns for principal security, plus the difficulties of improving benefits in the short term and providing disability benefits, all add up to less retirement income security.

However, a defined-contribution program may be designed to offset some of these weak points.

Control investments. As mentioned earlier, one of the biggest risks associated with defined-contribution plans comes from short-term fluctuations in the financial markets. Encourage investment strategies that emphasize guaranteed investment contracts, money market funds, or short-term bonds designed to guarantee preservation of principal.

Limit choice. Avoid arrangements that let participants select different types of investment programs that have a varying degree of risk. A retirement income program should not be a crap shoot.

Ensure disability provisions. Try to negotiate a long-term disability insurance program, separate from the retirement program, to provide disabled members with a certain amount of money each month for life.

Take care of older members. Target contributions to a desired benefit level, which means more will be contributed for the older participant. For example, in order to provide $100 a month at 6 percent interest over the life of the investment, a member who is 20 years old would need to make a contribution of roughly $4.50 a month, and the person 55 years old, $73.68. (Consulting Appendix D, divide the annual contribution by 12.)

Piggyback plans. Another approach to limiting the risks associated with defined-contribution plans is to have a basic defined-benefit plan for retirement security, piggybacked by a defined-contribution plan. However, this approach can cause difficulties in the long run, because when a retirement income vehicle that doesn't generate past service liability is available, companies will naturally concentrate on it at the bargaining table. As a result, your safety net—the defined-benefit plan—can become frayed by the fourth contract. This can be avoided if the union leadership makes sure that the defined-benefit program is adjusted during each negotiation.

5

The Defined-Benefit Plan: Benefits

No two pension plans are exactly alike. However, all defined-benefit plans have certain similarities. For example, all contain a method for calculating retirement benefits, all contain rules for determining who is eligible to receive benefits, and all contain language about how the plan will be administered.

As the possible combinations of benefits, eligibility rules, and administrative structures are nearly endless, this chapter will concentrate on the major benefits contained in a typical defined-benefit plan. Chapter 6 will concentrate on plan language.

The most important benefit, of course, is the monthly check your members will receive when they retire at the normal retirement age. This check is called the *normal retirement benefit*. The definition of "normal" varies from contract to contract.

Second in importance are provisions that allow the participant to retire earlier than the contract-defined normal time. These benefits typically are called *early retirement benefits* and, as with the normal retirement benefit, the definition of what constitutes "early" varies from contract to contract.

A third common benefit covers participants who become disabled before early or normal retirement age. Such *disability benefits* provide income from the time of the disability to the end of the worker's life.

Another standard benefit is the *preretirement surviving spouse benefit*. Before the passage of the Retirement Equity Act of 1984, every pension plan had to offer an active employee who attained early retirement eligibility the right to elect to have his or her surviving spouse covered should the employee die before actual retirement. As was mentioned in Chapter 2, REACT changed an employee's minimum eligibility for this benefit to the attainment of

43

vested status and made the benefit automatic. The important bargaining issues regarding this provision are who will pay for the benefit and how much the spouse will receive.

A final set of standard benefits concerns how the benefit is to be received. Most normal and early-retirement formulas state the benefit level in terms of *pure life annuities*, the monthly or yearly benefit the participant will receive for his or her lifetime, ceasing at death. All plans offer at least one alternative to this arrangement: the *50 percent surviving spouse option*, which means that the surviving spouse will receive 50 percent of the participant's reduced retirement income if the participant dies.

As you can see, the types of benefits in the typical plan are relatively few. There are several specific approaches to each, however.

The Normal Retirement Benefit

Every defined-benefit pension contract contains a formula for determining how much money a participant will get upon retirement. These formulas fall into four basic categories: *purely income-based, income and service, flat dollar and service,* and *flat dollar.*

Purely Income-Based Formulas

These are rare in negotiated plans, being almost always reserved for executive officers of major corporations. Such a formula might call for an individual to receive an annual pension equal to 50 percent of the person's final yearly salary. There is an implicit assumption that retirement income should be related to the standard of living one had achieved just before retirement. In the above example, the formula would result in a $50,000 annual pension for the $100,000-a-year executive, and $10,000 a year for the employee who retired at $20,000.

Income and Service Formulas

These share some characteristics of the income-based formulas in that the pension benefit will vary by level of average income. However, it also will vary by amount of credited service. A typical formula would be that "each participant will receive an annual retirement income equal to 1 percent of average income multiplied by the years of credited service accrued." (The 1 percent figure is used in this example to make calculations easier; many negotiated plans provide for a multiplier of 1.5 percent, 2 percent, or even 2.5 percent.) The definitional problems associated with average income and credited service will be discussed later in this chapter; although, as in the example below, a better-paid employee will receive a larger absolute pension, all participants receive the same pension relative to their salaries and years of service.

$$\text{Av. annual income} \times 1\% \times N \text{ years service} = \text{absolute pension}$$
$$\$12,000 \times 1\% \times 30 \text{ years} = \$3,600$$
$$\$18,000 \times 1\% \times 30 \text{ years} = \$5,400$$

The lower-paid participants pay the same price for food and other necessities as the higher-paid participants and, because they earned less throughout their work life, have had less opportunity to build a nest egg for retirement. Therefore, negotiating a minimum pension unrelated to income can help close the gap between the pensions earned by the highest- and lowest-paid workers.

Average earnings can be figured in a variety of ways: average annual income over the work life with the company, average yearly income in the final five years of work, or some variant. You can get an idea of how important this issue is from Tables 5-1 and 5-2. Based on a formula of 1 percent of career average earnings multiplied by a participant's years of service, the annual retirement benefit would be $2,325.69, which is not 1 percent × 30 years (30 percent of final yearly income), but only 13.5 percent. However, if the average income for the final five years is used as the average earnings figure, the benefit will be nearly twice as much: $4,542.35. This shows how similar formulas can result in benefit payouts which vary significantly depending on how average earnings are defined.

The best approach is to establish some type of final pay average, such as one based on annual pay during the last three to five years worked. Care must be taken to ensure that older workers are not penalized for bidding into less strenuous but lower-paying jobs, nor encouraged to work all the overtime they can to bump up their annual income. A way to guard against these situations is to provide a formula that averages the best five out of the last ten years, or the best three out of the last five.

An interesting feature of this sort of formula is that it has a built-in cost-of-living adjustment (COLA). Since the yearly benefit is tied to income, it will drift upward with increased hourly wages. To the extent that you are able to negotiate wage increases equal to or

Table 5-1. Hypothetical Annual Earnings over 30 Years for a Worker Employed in the Industrial Sector

1953	$3,664.44	1968	$ 6,370.52
1954	3,665.48	1969	6,734.52
1955	3,915.60	1970	6,933.16
1956	4,096.56	1971	7,406.88
1957	4,221.88	1972	8,044.92
1958	4,280.64	1973	8,655.92
1959	4,589.52	1974	9,193.60
1960	4,665.44	1975	9,921.08
1961	4,801.68	1976	10,884.64
1962	5,021.12	1977	11,902.80
1963	5,159.96	1978	12,962.04
1964	5,354.44	1979	14,005.68
1965	5,591.56	1980	15,008.24
1966	5,833.88	1981	16,536.00
1967	5,953.48	1982	$17,193.80

Table 5-2. Comparison of Career Average and Final Five-Year Average Plans Based on Wages in Table 5-1

	Career Average	Final Five-Year Average
Annual benefit	$2,325.69	$4,542.35
Monthly benefit	$193.80	$378.53
Percent of final yearly income replaced (annual benefit divided by final year's wages)	13.5%	26.4%
Effective $/month/year (monthly benefit divided by 30 years)	$6.46	$12.62

above the increase in the price rise (either through annual adjust-ments or automatic COLAs), your pension benefit will keep step with prices. There's a time lag, but it's better than no adjustment at all.

Variations on the income and service formula can either increase the disparity of the absolute pension levels or provide a minimum pension to counteract such disparities. For example, some pension plans have a formula which contains a tiered percent multiplier, such as 1 percent up to $7,800 of earnings, and 2 percent for any earnings above that level. You can see the impact of this if you study just one year's accumulation of benefits for two people, each with 30 years' service, but with substantially different wages: Harry, who earns $7,800 a year, and Estelle, who earns $15,000.

Harry: $7,800 × 1% = $78
Annual pension accumulation: $78
Relative pension: $78 × 30 = $2,340 (30% of annual wage)

Estelle: ($7,800 × 1% = $78) + ($7,200 × 2% = $144) = $222
Annual pension accumulation: $222
Relative pension: $222 × 30 = $6,660 (44% of annual wage)

Not only does the person with the higher income get a higher absolute pension, but the relative pension is higher as well.

As a negotiator, you also have to keep in mind that seemingly small changes in the percent multiplier translate into rather large increases in pension benefits. To go from 1 percent to 1.1 percent is not a .1 percent change; it's a 10 percent change.

$7,800 × .01 = $78, but $7,800 × .011 = $85.80, a 10% increase

Similarly, to move from a 1 percent multiplier to a 1.5 percent multiplier represents a 50 percent hike in the pension multiplier.

In tight economic times there will be pressure from the company to get rid of income and service plans. That's because the benefits fixed by the contract depend on wages in the future, wage scales which typically will be higher than current ones. This means that the actuary who is evaluating the plan's existing liabilities to be funded will take into account future benefit increases that automatically result from higher wages. The actuary will develop contribution recommendations on anticipated benefits, not current benefits, and this increases the current cost of the plan. This is not true of the dollar-per-month–per-year-of-service formulas. If the formula is currently $10 per month per year, the actuary assumes it will be the same 30 years from now and develops contribution recommendations based on current benefits rather than the higher future benefits.

Flat Dollar and Service Formulas

The most common formula in industrial contracts is based on service and a flat-dollar multiplier, such as $10 per month multiplied by the number of years of service (again, this $10 figure is used for illustrative purposes and does not constitute a recommendation). Under this formula a worker with 30 years of service would receive a monthly retirement benefit of $300. It makes no difference whether the retiree was making $5 an hour or $20 an hour before retirement; everyone gets the same benefit. This structure is based on the philosophy that retirement income should be based on need and, accordingly, lower-paid employees get a higher percentage of their income replaced in such a pension system than do higher-paid workers.

Union bargaining committees frequently ask if there is an ideal pension multiplier to aim for in a contract. Unfortunately, there isn't. The dollar multiplier varies all over the country depending on industry, location, plant, and local union. Some multipliers are around $20 a month per year of service, especially in industrywide contracts (auto, steel, and rubber, for example) or in plants that have been unionized for a long time. Other contracts contain multipliers as low as $2 a month per year of service; as one might guess, these are products of low-wage plants that have a relatively new union.

There are several variations to the flat dollar and service formula, and several issues that will come up at the bargaining table.

Because there is no recognition of income, some locals have found it necessary to bracket the multiplier by income level in an effort to recognize differing income levels. The UAW's master pension agreement with the auto industry contains four different multipliers according to income. When the unions negotiated a minimum pension formula to supplement the income and service formula at the Sperry Rand Corporation, the result was several multipliers bracketed by income. The bracket approach is a compromise between no recognition of income levels and exclusive dependence on income.

Negotiation of a long-term pension agreement (typically for three years) can itself raise problems. A typical pension settlement will call for a benefit to increase upon signing, with further increases in the second and third years of the contract. This sometimes encourages workers to put off retirement until the third year in order to get the maximum benefit, at which point they decide to hang on until the next contract to see if they can do even better. The negotiating committee may go to the table with a raft of workers just waiting for the ink to dry on the contract so they can retire. This can be a problem because the employer knows that any agreement regarding benefit increases will be payable immediately for a sizable group of people. This is costly because the interest discount, which would exist if contributions and interest were left to compound for a number of years, is lost.

A way to avoid this situation is to make all increases apply to any worker who retires under a given contract. For example, you've just negotiated an agreement that calls for a $1 increase in each of the three years of the contract. The current multiplier is $10. If you take the approach suggested here, you eliminate most of the incentive to defer retirement. When the benefit rate goes to $12 in the second year, everybody who retired at $11 the first year will receive the increase, and the same goes for the following year.

Another issue that has gained considerable attention at the bargaining table is the *future-service-only* provision. Typically, any negotiated benefit increase is applied to all years of service; however, in the 1980s companies have been attempting to negotiate increases that apply only to service that follows signing of the new agreement. This may save the company money, but it is not beneficial to the worker. A major goal of any negotiation is to help those who are about to retire or who will retire during the next contract. You will not help those people if you negotiate a future-service-only provision.

Further, this approach results in the same kind of problem that average income formulas create. You negotiate a future-service-only provision and you agree to a monthly benefit of $20 per year of service that might look good today, but won't necessarily look as good 30 years from now. Assuming a 6 percent inflation rate, the real value of $20 today will be $3.75 in 30 years. The problem is that workers earn pension benefits in accordance with prevailing wage levels and prices, but receive them in the future when things probably will be dramatically different. Future-service-only plans typically produce inadequate pension benefits. Companies push them because they are cheap, and they are cheap because they don't provide much in the way of benefits.

Flat Dollar Benefits

The fourth approach to figuring retirement income, the flat dollar benefit, is mainly of historical interest. Although flat dollar benefits were fairly common when unions first started to negotiate pensions (the first mine workers pension called for $100 a month, the first auto pension called for $100 a month including Social Security), this type of benefit exists today mostly in the disability area. Plans typically call for some dollar amount per year of service, with the provision that no one can get less than a minimum amount per month. The rationale is that disabling injuries or illnesses frequently occur early in the work life, and that some provision must be made for workers permanently removed from the work force.

Early Retirement Benefits

Most negotiated plans also provide for early retirement. Many of these early retirement programs grew out of industries where the work is, or was, physically demanding: including foundries, heavy equipment manufacturing, and mining. Workers in those industries often didn't want to risk waiting until age 65 to collect a pension because death and disability rates were so high. Other early retirement programs started out as jobs programs that enabled younger workers to advance more quickly because older workers could leave early. In other instances, early retirement programs were adopted merely because many people would rather do something else with their time than work.

It is important for negotiators to remember that early retirement programs don't spring up overnight. They are developed step-by-step, over a long period, by adding a small piece of the program with each contract. Further, your first priority is to provide a good normal retirement benefit. If your members can't retire comfortably at age 65 with a full benefit and unreduced Social Security, it is unlikely that an early retirement plan will offer any security.

The following section discusses early retirement programs from the simplest and least expensive through the more complex and costly.

Actuarial Reduction

While an early retirement program usually costs the plan money, programs may be designed that do not. These are plans that allow for retirement before the contract-specified normal age, at a full actuarial reduction in the normal benefit for each month that an individual retires ahead of the normal age.

A *full actuarial reduction* is a reduction in the normal benefit that is just large enough to offset the cost increase which results when an individual leaves ahead of schedule. There is a cost increase because an individual who retires early receives benefits for a longer period of time, causing the fund to pay out money on which it could be earning interest.

For example, according to the mortality tables a male who retires at age 55 rather than 65 will live, and receive benefits, for 24 more years. Had he retired at age 65, he probably would have received benefits for only 15 years. So if he were to receive the full retirement benefit ($100 per month, for this example) for 24 years, he would cost the plan $28,800 ($100 a month × 12 × 24 years = $28,800) rather than the $18,000 he would have cost the plan had he retired at age 65 ($100 a month × 12 × 15 years = $18,000). The $10,800 difference represents a 60 percent increase in expenditure, not to mention the forgone interest.

A reasonable rule of thumb is that it costs a plan up to 8 percent more for each year a person retires ahead of the normal retirement age. Therefore, if an annuity costs $11,654.40 at age 65 for a benefit of $100 a month for life, it would cost $932.35 more ($11,654.40 × .08 = $932.35) at age 64. Rather than pay this cost, many plans simply reduce the normal retirement benefit by enough to offset the cost increase. In the example, the normal benefit of $100 a month would be reduced by the amount of the cost increase (8 percent) to $92. Although the individual is receiving retirement income for a longer period of time, the value of the total expected payments is roughly equal. This benefit reduction of $8 is the actuarial reduction.

The first step in developing an early retirement program is to replace the words "actuarial reduction" with a specific, contractually agreed-upon number, such as 7 or 8 percent. If you negotiate an 8 percent per year reduction and the full actuarial reduction is already 8 percent a year, you haven't done much in the way of improving benefits. However, you've set the stage for the next round of negotiations; it is much easier to negotiate on the size of a specific number than to negotiate over a principle. Go carefully, however; one major problem you must look out for is how the reduction is calculated. Examine Table 5–3, in which both schedules follow a 7 percent per year reduction in a $100 a month benefit.

The difference is that the rate is compounded downward in Method A by taking 7 percent of the previous year's benefit rather than returning to the normal retirement base for each year's calculation. Method B, which works off the normal retirement base, is the more common in negotiated plans. There is not much difference in the plans in the years immediately before age 65 (at 62, for instance, the difference is only $1.44 a month) but by age 55 the difference is nearly $20 a month. Of course, one can argue that anyone who retires at age 55 must have other sources of income and therefore it's hard to be too concerned about the fate of such a porkchopper; however, bear in mind that some people are more or less forced to retire early, including those who are out of work because of a plant closing, and those whose health is too poor for them to keep up with their job demands but who still don't meet the terms of the disability pension.

When you go from full actuarial reduction to a specific table in your pension plan, try to get an agreement that the specific rate will be compounded downward as illustrated in Table 5–3, Method A.

Make certain in going from full actuarial reductions to specific rates that no one is penalized as a result of the change. This can

---

Table 5-3. Effects of Different Methods of Actuarial Reduction on a Normal Retirement Benefit of $100

Age	Method A 7% per Year Compounded Downward	Method B 7% per Year from Normal Retirement Base
65	$100.00	$100.00
64	93.00	93.00
63	86.49	86.00
62	80.44	79.00
61	74.81	72.00
60	69.57	65.00
59	64.70	58.00
58	60.17	51.00
57	55.96	44.00
56	52.05	37.00
55	48.40	30.00

happen if the actuary has been using sex-segregated tables to calculate the actuarial reduction factors. Since women as a class live longer (by about five years), insurance carriers and actuaries have traditionally placed a higher value on their monthly retirement benefits, because women as a class will collect for a longer period of time. (As with any actuarial table, an individual woman's mortality will probably differ substantially from the group's characteristics.) Therefore, the relative increase in cost to the plan of a female retiring early as opposed to a male is smaller, and the associated actuarial reduction is smaller. In the past, in plans that called for an actuarial reduction for early retirement, it was not unusual to see actuarial reductions which were considerably smaller for female participants.

[*Author's Comment*—The issue of actuarial tables segregated by sex probably will disappear in the years to come as a result of the 1983 U.S. Supreme Court decision, *Brown v. Arizona*, which made it illegal for an employer to offer annuity options that pay less to female employees based on their longer mortality as a class.

Unfortunately, the case dealt with a defined-contribution plan rather than a defined-benefit plan, so the issue decided was not identical to the one above. However, if the Court's logic is applied to the early retirement issue, it would be reasonable to conclude that differing early retirement benefits based on sex violate the law. What the Court did not specify was how to solve the problem.

There are three probable solutions, as seen in the example of a male and a female both retiring under the same plan at age 62. The plan pays $100 a month at age 65, with a 7 percent per year reduction for males who retire early and a 4 percent per year reduction for females.

	Male Benefit	Female Benefit
Current:	$79/month	$88 month
Solution A:	$79/month	$79/month (lower hers to his)
Solution B:	$83.50/month	$83.50/month (raise his, lower hers, splitting the difference)
Solution C:	$88/month	$88 month (raise his to hers)

Unfortunately, the Supreme Court did not say which of the three solutions is correct. If the courts decide in future years that Solution C is the answer, there will be no problem. However,

Solutions A and B represent a loss in benefits for the female workers, and if either of these are allowed in court, then unions will have to negotiate Solution C at the bargaining table.—J. MacD.]

The next step in developing an early retirement program, which probably will take place in contract talks some time after you've negotiated the initial rate, is to work on reducing the specific reduction factor. Put your efforts where they will count the most. Unless your members have some other source of income, they'll start to consider early retirement only when they are eligible for early Social Security, about age 62. Your first efforts should be to reduce the reduction factor for the three years from age 62 through age 65, with the eventual goal being no reduction at all after age 62.

Health Insurance

Probably as important as reduction factors in an individual's decision to retire early is the availability of health insurance coverage. Since Medicare coverage starts at age 65, members under age 65 who retire have no health insurance coverage unless it is provided by contract or unless they are able to buy their own coverage. Eliminating the reduction factor is a minor savings compared to the high monthly costs of individual health insurance premiums, if the individual can even get private health care coverage. Therefore, any local seriously concerned about an early retirement program should negotiate for contract proposals that ensure health care coverage for early retirees.

Social Security Supplement

The next step often is to compensate high-service members for the lack of Social Security prior to age 62. This can be quite expensive—so expensive, in fact, that you should first consider whether the benefit is worth the cost in other wage and fringe benefits forgone, including a higher normal retirement benefit. If you decide it is worth the cost, *30-and-out*, which allows workers to retire after 30 years' service, regardless of age, is one approach to take. This approach derived from early retirement programs in industries in which workers often became disabled after long years of service. Hanging on for a full, unreduced pension at the normal retirement age was almost meaningless. In those shops, unions pushed hard to negotiate 30-and-out programs.

There are two ways to set up 30-and-out programs. The first provides a supplement which, when added to the reduced normal retirement benefits, raises the benefit to a fixed number of dollars per month. This supplement is intended to approximate the value of Social Security at age 62; it usually lasts only for those years from actual retirement to age 62, when the supplement stops and Social Security kicks in to provide a reasonable level of income over a retiree's lifetime.

The second approach gives a retirement supplement of x dollars a month per year of service to an individual who has more than 30 years. For example, one Sperry Vickers plan called for a $3.25 supplement per month per year of service for all workers who retired with more than 30 years' service.

Most 30-and-out or other retirement income supplement programs have earnings limitations similar to those attached to receiving Social Security benefits. The historical reasons for these limitations are twofold. First, companies didn't want a 48-year-old worker to take a 30-and-out pension and go down the road to work for a competitor; second, these expensive programs are for workers who want or need to *retire*, not workers who want to continue working with a second source of income.

Surviving Spouse Benefits

One of the most difficult things to explain—and to justify— under a defined-benefit plan is why, when a participant dies, his or her beneficiary does not "inherit" the accumulated benefit. The reason is that a pension plan provides income to *retirees*, not to the families of retirees. Death benefits are not the concern of a pension plan and are, or should be, provided through negotiated life insurance coverage. However, the rationale for the lack of death benefits sounds hollow when you're talking with the spouse of a long-service member who had worked at a shop where the life insurance had been deficient. There have been two attempts to partially rectify this situation.

Preretirement Surviving Spouse Coverage

One solution was to include in ERISA the requirement that qualified pension plans offer preretirement surviving spouse coverage, which provides that an active employee who reaches early retirement eligibility be offered the right to elect to cover his or her spouse under the pension plan so that if the employee dies while actively employed, the surviving spouse will receive 50 percent of the pension, calculated as though the employee had retired the day the death occurred. If the employee does not elect the coverage, the spouse doesn't get anything.

The inclusion of this requirement certainly was an improvement over the time when plans were not required to offer anything. However, the requirement had a cost attached to it, because the law allows plans to charge for the benefit of coverage, typically .7 percent or .8 percent for each year the coverage is in effect. Therefore, an individual who elects coverage at age 55 and who retires at age 65 (that is, with 10 years' coverage) would have his or her accumulated pension reduced 7 or 8 percent by the actual retirement date. For someone with 30 years' service and a $10 pension multiplier at age 65, the normal unreduced pension would be $300 a month and the benefit with the preretirement surviving spouse election would be 7 percent less, or $279 ($300 × .93 = $279).

The problem with this approach is not that it is a prohibitive cost, but that it puts people in the position of trying to predict their mortality, something few people are good at. The result is that some people who don't elect this coverage in order to maintain higher benefits at age 65 die before retirement, leaving their spouses without an income.

A negotiator should remember two important points: offering the preretirement surviving spouse benefit is a *minimum* standard, and who makes the contribution for this benefit is negotiable. Every union should try to negotiate an automatic preretirement surviving spouse benefit without reductions. This eliminates the election, so that every married worker who reaches early retirement eligibility will be covered by this benefit.

Further, note that the benefit is attached to early retirement *eligibility*. You should consider improving the early retirement eligibility requirements not because you think many will retire early but to get the preretirement surviving spouse coverage. A number of negotiated plans still require the participant to reach age 60 with 10 years' service for early retirement eligibility. Therefore, a 58-year-old with 38 years' service is not eligible for coverage. You might attempt to negotiate retirement eligibility at age 55 or 30 years' service so that individuals in this situation will at least have the opportunity to cover their spouses. You also can negotiate coverage higher than 50 percent, including 100 percent, for surviving spouses.

REACT expanded ERISA requirements on preretirement spouse benefits. Under ERISA the pension plan only had to offer a preretirement spouse benefit and there was no requirement that the spouse be involved in the decision to elect or reject the coverage. REACT makes the preretirement surviving spouse coverage automatic, that is, the employee is covered unless he or she specifically waives the coverage in writing. Further, the employee must have the written consent of the spouse to waive the benefit.

In addition, REACT made the automatic preretirement spouse coverage effective when an employee becomes vested rather than when an employee reaches early retirement eligibility, as was the case under ERISA. Therefore, an employee who became vested under a pension plan at, for example, age 38 would automatically be covered by a surviving spouse benefit unless both the employee and spouse elected not to be covered by the benefit. Should the employee subsequently die, his or her spouse would be eligible to begin collecting a pension benefit at the time the employee would have otherwise reached early retirement age.

Many negotiating issues, however, were not significantly altered under REACT, mainly (1) who will pay for the surviving spouse benefit and (2) what will be the level of the surviving spouse benefit. As under ERISA, the plan is allowed to shift the cost of this benefit to the plan participant by actuarially reducing the eventual early or normal retirement benefit. Many contracts provide that there will be no benefit reduction suffered as a result of this coverage. Further, the law only provides that the surviving spouse will receive 50 percent of the employee's accrued pension benefit. This is a minimum legal requirement and many negotiated contracts considerably improve on this, some providing 66 percent or 80 percent of the accrued pension benefit.

Automatic Joint-and-Survivor Coverage

The second improvement that ERISA made in surviving spouse benefits was mandating that defined-benefit pension plans make a joint-and-survivor annuity (rather than an automatic straight or pure-life annuity) the normal form of annuity for participants married over one year.

An *annuity* is simply a promise to make periodic payments, such as once a year or once a month, to a designated person for a designated period of time. The pension benefit formulas contained In defined-benefit pensions typically are stated in the straight life or annuity form; for example, a contract calls for $10 per month per year of service payable to the participant for his or her life. When the participant dies, the promise liquidates; neither the spouse nor any other designated beneficiary has a claim on the promise. Before the passage of ERISA this was the typical automatic benefit; if a worker did not elect another form of benefit this was the annuity he or she received. However, most plans offered at least one option in the form of a joint-and-survivor annuity, which paid a reduced benefit to the participant and spouse until both were dead, with the surviving spouse receiving a percentage of the participant's pension, usually one half or two thirds.

The problem was that before ERISA the participant was faced with a choice that amounted to gambling with his or her mortality; individuals frequently did not elect spouse coverage. Why? Because when an individual elects such coverage the monthly annuity is reduced to reflect the cost associated with providing the benefit for the length of two lives rather than one, and typical reductions might be 15 percent or higher, depending on the age of the spouse. On a $350 monthly annuity, for example, that could mean a reduction of $52.50 a month to cover the contingency that he or she may not survive the spouse. That's $630 a year less, nearly two month's worth of unreduced annuity.

On the theory that people are more apt to exercise a negative option (do nothing) than a positive option (do something), ERISA mandated that participants would have to make a conscious decision *not* to cover their spouses by so informing the plan administrator. However, the law did not eliminate the actuarial adjustments from the straight life associated with the different annuity forms. Further, a majority of negotiated contracts simply call for actuarial adjustments from the straight life annuity for the "50 percent J&S," as it's called. As indicated previously, these adjustments can be quite substantial, depending on the age of the spouse. The larger the reduction is, the larger the incentive is to elect straight life. Because of this adverse incentive, many union negotiators try to place specific limits on the amount of reductions for the 50 percent J&S, with the expectation that in subsequent negotiations the limits on the reductions will be further reduced until they are entirely eliminated.

Straight life annuity forms and the 50 percent joint-and-survivor benefit are the basic forms contained in all union contracts. However, there are additional forms that can be negotiated.

Life annuities certain and continuous guarantee that a certain number of monthly payments will be made regardless of whether the participant lives or dies, with the promise that the payment will continue for life. The guaranteed payments can be for any number of months, but typically run 60 months (five years) or 120 months (ten years). The monthly payment actually received will be lower than that provided under the straight life annuity.

Refund annuities guarantee a return to the surviving spouse of the unused portion of the purchase price or value of the annuity.

Having a wide range of annuity options certainly increases the flexibility of a retiring participant's financial planning, although more than two or three basic options probably add to the anxiety of the decision without significant positive benefits.

Summary

It is easy to think up superficially appealing proposals in the benefits area. However, as a negotiator, you should recognize that until the basic benefit at normal retirement is adequate, success in other areas is an empty promise. Don't be like the local that put most of its bargaining power behind a 30-and-out retirement program when the basic benefit at normal retirement was only $3.50 per month per year of service. That's putting the proverbial cart before the horse.

6

The Defined-Benefit Plan: Language

It is largely an artificial distinction to consider pension plan benefits and language separately. In one sense, all of a pension plan is a matter of language, even the normal retirement benefit. However, the distinction makes sense in terms of the attention language usually gets at the bargaining table. Nearly every contract negotiation has a proposal for improving the retirement benefit multiplier; less frequently discussed are how to define time in service, what constitutes "normal" retirement, and what powers a plan administrator has during a plan termination.

Pension language does not have much intrinsic interest for the rank and file. Few members even read the summary plan description until they retire, if then. Therefore, a ground swell of grassroots support for pension language changes is rare. However, language can make the difference between an average pension plan and a fine plan that meets the needs of your members.

Because each pension plan is unique, it is nearly impossible to cover all the language issues that could come up during a negotiation. However, the more important areas can be dealt with by walking a typical new member through her work life to point out the major areas of concern to members, and by examining the less visible areas that should concern the bargaining committee. Detailed discussions of each area follow the overview.

How Pension Language Affects Members

Franceen Yoder hires in as a new employee. After serving a short probation, she is covered by all aspects of the collective bargaining agreement, including the grievance procedure, holiday pay, and health insurance.

When is she covered by the pension agreement? She can find out by looking at the section of the summary plan description covering *participation rules.*

Now that she's a participant, her next major concern is how she accumulates time toward her retirement eligibility and how benefits are calculated. *Service counting rules* determine these matters.

If Franceen is laid off, how long does she have before she is terminated from the plan? If she's called back, will she come back as a new employee? *Break-in-service rules* govern these situations.

How much service will she need in order to keep her retirement benefits if she quits or gets fired? *Vesting rules* answer these questions.

When is she eligible to receive the disability, early retirement, or normal retirement benefits discussed in Chapter 5. *Benefit eligibility rules* cover these issues.

Most contract language will involve the five above areas. Three additional areas affect the plan itself, including:

- *Plan administration* (This encompasses who will run the plan, how it will be run, and what powers the administrator has.)
- *Plan funding* (Although ERISA comprehensively covers pension funding, union contracts can have requirements that are stricter than ERISA's.)
- *Plan amendment or modification* (ERISA also contains participant protection to cover pension plan terminations. However, this is only minimum protection, and unions can negotiate more comprehensive protection.)

Participation

A major part of a pension plan is the language that describes who can become a member of the group making up the plan. The participation section of the contract is especially important because a member doesn't start accumulating service until he or she is a participant.

The criteria typically used to determine an individual's right to participate are *age* and *length of service* with an employer or industry.

Before the enactment of ERISA, participation was strictly limited, particularly in nonunion plans. An individual might be required to wait up to 10 years and reach age 35 before being admitted to participation. This created problems: many workers either never became participants because of job quits or terminations, or were unable to accumulate an adequate benefit because of the late starting date.

The situation improved under ERISA as amended by the Retirement Equity Act. The most a plan can now require for participation is attainment of age 21 or one year of service, whichever comes later. This is an improvement, although it prevents someone who starts work right out of high school from accumulating benefits for a couple of years.

The bargaining goal regarding participation language is to treat a pension like any other benefit: when members complete their probationary periods, they should begin to participate. For all practical purposes, workers should begin to participate immediately.

Service Accrual

Franceen has served her probationary period and now is participating in the pension plan. She doesn't gain much beyond the right to participate. Her eventual right to a pension and its size will depend on her length of service with the employer. On the surface, this would seem a simple matter to determine—her participation began January 1 of one year, and 30.5 years later, when she retires, she will have 30.5 years of service. But, as one might suspect, it's not that simple. How an individual acquires a year of service, or additional years of service, is determined by the wording of the pension plan document.

How service is determined is one of the most complex areas of any pension program, and one of the more difficult areas of ERISA to understand. First, there are two basic approaches to counting service that satisfy ERISA—elapsed-time systems and hours-counting systems; second, within each of these systems there are usually two types of service—service toward vesting and benefit eligibility, and service toward benefit accumulation, i.e., the service that is multiplied by the basic benefit rate.

The potential for confusion is great. Most negotiated plans pick one service counting system and use that system to determine vesting and eligibility service as well as benefit service. Unfortunately, many other plans use one system for vesting and another for benefit accumulation. The result is messy and confusing.

The basics of the two approaches are explained below. The intent is not to cover the topic comprehensively but rather to identify the most common areas of bargaining concern. To find out how any given plan actually operates in this area, the negotiator must meet with the plan administrator to study specific examples of members employed at differing levels of age and service who have experienced differing types of absences from work. Such a study will identify the impact of such absences on hours and service accrual.

Elapsed Time

The *elapsed-time* method is the closest to the typical seniority method of counting time. Simply stated, it is determined by subtracting the worker's hire-in date from his or her termination date. As long as there continues to be an employment relationship between employee and employer, service continues to accrue. This is a simple system because it is unnecessary to count the hours actually worked or compensated. From the company's point of view, it is easy to administer; from the worker's point of view, it is easy to understand. When Franceen retires, it is clear why she has 30.5 years of service credited to her pension.

Determining when a participant's service terminates is the major bargaining issue in an elapsed-time setup. If one of your members pokes a foreman in the nose and gets fired, this individual has clearly terminated the relationship with the employer. When someone quits to take a new job, it's again a clear-cut termination of the employment relationship.

But what about an illness that requires a worker to take medical leave for one and one-half years? What about indefinite layoff with recall rights for as long as a worker has seniority? During the 1982–83 recession, workers with as much as 25 years of service were laid off indefinitely, and because of their contracts had recall rights for up to 25 years. Did they continue to accrue pension service during that time? If so, what type of service—benefit, vesting, or both?

To say they continue to accrue pension service is easy, but there's a problem, as illustrated by the case of an auto parts supplier that started as a munitions plant employing over 1,000 people during World War II. Because of demographic, technological, and market changes after the plant moved into auto parts in the postwar period, the plant today has a permanent work force of just over 100 employees. At the time of the most recent negotiations, there were 102 active employees accumulating service under the plan, and more than 200 on layoff, some of whom were still accumulating service although they had not worked at the plant for more than 10 years. The cost of the pension plan at that plant was astronomical because only one out of three people accumulating benefits was working—a good deal for those on layoff but an impossible situation for a bargaining committee trying to improve the pensions of the people still in the shop.

It's important to review the contract to determine how long service will continue to accumulate when an individual has an employment relationship but is not being compensated either directly through wages or indirectly through sickness and accident or long-term disability insurance. In most labor agreements, limits on service accumulations are more restrictive than recall rights. ERISA does not set limits, but it does set a 12-month minimum standard for service accrual on layoff.

Many pension agreements distinguish between a year of service for calculating benefits and a year of service for benefit eligibility and vesting. The service-counting rules for benefit eligibility and vesting are usually much more liberal than those that determine benefit accrual. That's because eligibility for a benefit does not come in gradations; you are either 100 percent eligible or not eligible at all. And while a five-year loss of credit may mean a decrease in the monthly benefit you receive, loss of a single year's credit toward eligibility may mean complete forfeiture of the pension.

Under many negotiated elapsed-time methods, a participant taking an approved leave of absence would accumulate more service toward benefit eligibility and vesting than toward benefit accumulation. For example: Franceen's labor contract provides up to five years toward eligibility if she goes on indefinite layoff, but she will accumulate only 12 months' worth of benefits in those five years. If she works five years and goes on indefinite layoff the next five years, she will have 10 years of service toward benefit eligibility at the end of the second five-year period, and be vested according to the contract; however, she stopped accumulating benefits at the end of the first 12 months of layoff (after the sixth year of the employment relationship), so she would be vested for six years of benefits rather than 10. Six years, however, is better than being vested for no years at all.

Hours Counting

A method used more frequently than elapsed time is the *hours-counting method*, which designates a certain number of hours worked in a 12-month period as a year toward either eligibility or benefit credit. In almost all cases the number of hours needed within a 12-month period is less for vesting and benefit eligibility credit than for benefit accumulation credit.

The vesting service standard typically is 1,000 hours in a 12-month period, one of several minimum standards allowed by ERISA. The hours for one year of benefit accumulation run between 1,600 and 1,800 in most plants.

Hours counting is clearly a more complex method than elapsed time, and one less subject to membership scrutiny. While a worker often remembers an extended layoff that happened 20 years ago, it's unusual for someone to remember with accuracy how many hours he or she worked the year before.

Further, the definition of "hour" matters much more in the hours-counting approach. An hour of work is usually defined as an hour for which an employee is directly compensated through wages, vacation, or holiday pay, or indirectly compensated through a private insurance program such as short-term disability. Indirectly compensated hours, however, frequently are limited to the ERISA minimum of 501 hours. Most short-term disability programs provide income payments for up to 1,040 hours (26 weeks), with the result that a worker can lose up to 539 hours toward pension eligibility and vesting by exercising sickness and accident rights under the contract. That's only one third of a 1,500-hour year, but it can be an important third.

Take the case of Larry Wilson, who becomes disabled in an auto accident just after completing his ninth year of work. He goes on short-term disability for 26 weeks and, because of the seriousness of his injury, can't come back to work. He has credit for 501 hours by ERISA standards in the year he was injured, but to be vested at the end of his 10th year, he would need 1,000 hours (the ERISA minimum) or more. If all compensated hours are counted, he will receive credit for 1,040 hours; however, if his plan allows only the ERISA minimum of 501 indirectly compensated hours, he will not become vested.

While the likelihood of this happening is slim, keep in mind that pensions cover large numbers of people. Anything that can happen probably will. When it does, it's too late to change the plan to help one unfortunate person.

Remember that what constitutes an hour under this system is negotiable, as long as the minimums are met. If Larry Wilson's union had negotiated full crediting of hours for workers receiving benefits under the short-term disability program, Wilson would have been eligible for a disability pension or a *deferred vested pension* (the normal or early retirement pension provided to vested participants who separate from service before the early retirement eligibility date) if he were not able to return to work.

The definition of what is and what is not an hour under an hours-counting system can have a dramatic effect on benefit amounts. The actual number of hours needed for one full year of benefit service varies considerably from one contract to another but, as mentioned above, usually falls in a range of 1,600 to 1,800 hours. Service is often prorated for fewer hours worked, so that if an employee works half of a normal year (e.g., 900 hours out of 1,800), he or she receives credit for .5 years. The important thing to remember is that the hours requirement should be negotiated at such a level that full-time workers who take normal amounts of time off should receive a full year's service.

For example, your contract designates 1,700 hours as one year of benefit service. Just before negotiations begin, you check the credited service for your members and find that a substantial number of full-time employees are receiving less than a full year's credit for a year of work. Your hours requirement is probably too high for your industry. There's no "right" or "wrong" figure to aim for—it's a question of what works to generate a full year's service for a full year's work. If your hours count doesn't do that, the figure should be reduced to a more appropriate level.

The flip side is the issue of crediting more than one year's service during a 12-month period. If the hours requirement is 1,700 hours for a full year, and a participant is credited with 1,870 hours, should the participant then be credited with 1.1 years of service? Some pensions do, but there are pitfalls.

Such an arrangement sets up a perverse incentive system that tends to coerce the participant into working increasingly longer hours as he or she gets older. As workers near retirement age, many will try to work more than a normal workweek in order to increase pension income. Do you want to promote this? Probably not, because the best way to improve monthly retirement benefits is to increase the basic benefit, not to manipulate the hours requirement.

Locals will sometimes be tempted by this approach in order to disguise what amounts to a basic benefit improvement. When nearly everyone is being credited with 1.1 years on a $10 multiplier, it's roughly the same as having an $11 multiplier with a maximum of one year's service. Why not just go for the extra $1?

The larger problem with an hours-counting system is in the area of layoffs longer than a few weeks. An ongoing employment relationship exists but, because the worker is not being compensated either directly or indirectly through a privately sponsored insurance program, he or she is not being credited with hours toward benefit accumulation or vesting service. The severity of the problem varies by plant, industry, and the general state of the economy.

Although ERISA overlooked the impact of layoffs on yearly benefit accumulation, as a negotiator you should not. There are two basic approaches. One is to reduce the number of hours needed to accumulate one year of service, as by lowering the requirement from 1,800 to 1,650 hours for benefit accumulation, or from 1,000 to 750 hours for vesting service.

The other approach is to credit hours for time while on layoff, up to certain limits. The United Auto Workers' master agreements with the major auto companies provide that an individual who works 170 hours in a plan year is eligible for up to 11 additional months' service while on layoff.

Breaks in Service and Severance from Service

Once a member becomes a participant and accumulates service, the next issue concerns breaks in service under the pension plan. The issue is similar to breaks in seniority—both exist because of the nature of work in our economy. Although some people work for the same employer for years without interruption, others' work relationships will be interrupted through illness, indefinite layoff, military obligations, or family responsibilities. While the central concern of the labor contract is the impact these interruptions have on job rights, the pension document is concerned with the circumstances under which a participant loses accumulated benefits because of a separation from work.

In the pension agreement, provisions concerning continuity of pension rights are found under the break-in-service or severance-from-service sections and in the vesting section.

Under ERISA, an unvested participant generally loses accumulated pension rights by becoming separated from work for a period that is longer than the period worked. This is called the *parity rule.* If Franceen Yoder had participated for six years, gone on indefinite layoff for the next seven years, then come back to work, it would be permissible under the law for the employer to bring her back as a new employee. REACT modified the parity rule by additionally providing that an individual with less than five years' vesting service could not break service until he or she had at least five consecutive one-year breaks in service. Anyone with more than five years of service toward vesting would come under the parity rule. An additional provision is that a worker must be credited with at least 501 hours of service for time on maternity or paternity leave.

As with benefits accumulation, the two approaches to measuring breaks in service are hours counting and elapsed time.

Under the hours-counting method, an employee who works fewer than 501 hours in a 12-month period is considered to have a one-year break in service. A one-year break is not overly important for pension purposes unless you have only one year of participation. However, if the number of consecutive years with fewer than 501 hours is greater than the accumulated years of vesting service under the plan, an unvested participant loses any claim to pension benefits.

The 501-hours figure ties into the service-counting system under the ERISA definition of hours because a plan has to credit at least 501 hours of a paid absence, most notably for a short-term disability. Therefore, it's impossible for a worker to break service when he or she is on sickness and accident leave, or on any other leave of absence that is paid directly or indirectly.

Under the elapsed-time method, an individual is considered to have a one-year break in service if he or she does not receive one hour of compensation within a 12-month period.

Break-in-service rules are fairly standard. Most contracts follow the parity rule or improve it slightly. The major differences come either in hours credited on approved leaves of absence or in the definition of severance from service under the elapsed-time approach.

Vesting

In a dynamic economy it is not uncommon for people to change jobs fairly often, and few people actually spend their entire work lives with one firm. Further, regardless of liberal parity rules, many people do not come back to a job once they've left, whether voluntarily or involuntarily. If pension eligibility were protected solely by break in service rules, most people would never receive a pension—hence the establishment of *vesting*. Vesting permits a worker to terminate service at some point in the work life, regardless of cause, without endangering the benefit that has accumulated to that date.

Vesting was well established in labor contracts long before ERISA established minimum standards for all qualified pension plans. Today, the most common vesting standard found in industrial union contracts calls for *10-year cliff vesting*, which means that after 10 years of vesting service a worker becomes 100 percent vested in his or her accumulated benefit. The "cliff" refers to the fact that on one day a worker has no vesting at all, and on the next, the worker is completely vested. There is no gradation of eligibility.

Cliff vesting can cause great disparity of treatment under a plan. Two people with roughly the same service can receive glaringly different benefits. The disparity is not as obvious when employment is relatively stable and job prospects are good, because individuals can voluntarily adjust their work relationships and terminations to avoid sudden losses. If a person has nine years' service it makes sense to hang on for an extra 1,000 hours of work to get in 10 years. On the other hand, the positive aspects of the job change could outweigh the loss of accumulated pension benefits. The key is the voluntary nature of the decision. However, voluntary job choices are almost exclusively associated with a healthy industry and strong general economy.

The arbitrary nature of 10-year cliff vesting is especially obvious and painful when a plant closes or where there is a substantial level of indefinite or permanent layoffs. These involuntary separations from work frequently involve forfeitures of substantial benefits. In just about every case there are one or more workers who were short just a few hours and who are now permanently excluded from the pension they had been counting on.

A way to soften the cliff effects of 10-year vesting is to use *graded vesting*, which means a participant gets a certain percent of the benefit vested each year. As one might imagine, the type of grading can vary considerably. The two most common types in negotiated contracts are *5-to-15-year grading*, which is provided as an option under ERISA, and the preferable *5-to-10-year grading*.

Table 6–1. Comparison of Graded Vesting Methods

5-to-15-Year Grading		5-to-10-Year Grading	
Years of Service	% Vested	Years of Service	% Vested
5	25%	5	50%
6	30%	6	60%
7	35%	7	70%
8	40%	8	80%
9	45%	9	90%
10	50%	10	100%
11	60%		
12	70%		
13	80%		
14	90%		
15	100%		

In terms of protection, 5-to-10-year graded vesting obviously is better than 10-year cliff vesting, but depending on industry turnover patterns, the 5-to-15 year plan might provide less security than 10-year cliff. In the health industry, for example, turnover is usually high, so graded vesting makes more sense than 10-year cliff vesting. However, in public utilities, where turnover is less frequent, 10-year cliff vesting might provide greater benefit security. Auto parts supply, once a stable industry with a fairly secure job environment, now is beset by layoffs and frequent plant relocations. The typical 10-year cliff system is no longer well suited to this industry.

There is one other major form of vesting schedule: *age and service vesting*. The formula allowed under ERISA provides that an individual who has five years' service, and whose age plus five years equals 45 or 46, will be vested according to the schedule in Table 6–2. However, this schedule, which is known as the *Rule of 45*, has an additional requirement: that the schedule shown in Table 6–3 must apply to any individual who has 10 or more years of service regardless of age.

Vesting represents one of the few instances in which a defined-contribution plan is superior to a defined-benefit plan, because the former almost always provides for 100 percent vesting after a short period, in many cases immediately upon participation.

Table 6–2. The Rule of 45

Years of Service	Sum of Age and Service	Percent Vested
5	45 or 46	50%
6	47 or 48	60%
7	49 or 50	70%
8	51 or 52	80%
9	53 or 54	90%
10	55 or more	100%

Of course, the more liberal vesting requirements are, the more expensive pension costs will be, because certain *turnover discounts* (savings that result from employee turnover) are eliminated. It is possible, though, that the example of defined-contribution plans will cause labor negotiators to review traditional vesting concepts and attempt to liberalize plans to make them more competitive in this arca and to appeal to younger members.

Benefit Eligibility

As discussed earlier in Chapter 5, the different benefits a pension may offer are limited: normal retirement, early retirement,

Table 6–3. Required Vesting Regardless of Age

Years of Service	Percent Vested
10	50%
11	60%
12	70%
13	80%
14	90%
15	100%

disability retirement, deferred vested, and preretirement surviving spouse. Once an individual becomes a participant, service accumulates not only for the calculation of the retirement benefit amount and toward vesting but for eligibility to actually receive the benefit. Most pensions have a service requirement for the eligibility to receive the benefit. For example, a pension plan might have an early retirement eligibility requirement of age 55 and 15 years of "service." Service could refer to vesting service, which for purposes of discussion might be one year of service if a plan participant is credited with 1000 hours in a plan year (zero years if less than 1000 hours). Alternatively, service could refer to the crediting service for benefit calculation which might call for .1 of a benefit credit for each 180 hours. It's easy to see that these two service counting approaches frequently have different results, as shown in the following examples:

A. A plan participant is credited with 900 hours in a plan year. He or she would be credited with .5 of a year (900 ÷ 180 × .1) for the purpose of benefit calculation and zero years of vesting service.

B. A plan participant works 1080 hours in a plan year. He or she would be credited with .6 of a year (1080 ÷ 180 × .1) for the purpose of benefit calculation and one full year of vesting service.

These two examples illustrate how a plan participant can accumulate different amounts of "service" in one year and conceivably be eligible for a benefit under the service used for benefit calculation and not be eligible under the service accumulation rules used for vesting, or the reverse.

In the area of benefit eligibility it is wise to negotiate for a system that favors the individual over the plan. Therefore, the better plans state eligibility rules in terms of either vesting or benefit service, whichever is greater. If a worker qualifies under either rule, he or she is eligible.

Plan Administration

With the exception of multiemployer Taft-Hartley plans, which are trusteed by a joint union-management committee, union leaders and negotiators rarely are involved in questions of plan administration except on a case-by-case basis. However, there are two related areas of importance that deserve attention: pension dispute resolution and joint union-company pension committees.

Pension Dispute Resolution

The grievance is the time-honored dispute resolution procedure in labor relations, with either the right to strike or to go to arbitration as the final step. Unfortunately, many labor agreements still preclude taking pension disputes to arbitration. How, then, are pension disputes resolved?

ERISA requires every pension plan to have a procedure for resolving disputes, but does not specify that the procedure must include a neutral third party. The result is that the person with whom the union is disagreeing often is the one who rules on the matter. This is obviously an undesirable situation. If a participant is unhappy with the eventual decision of the internal procedure, the Department of Labor can be asked to investigate; eventually, the dispute can end up in court. At best, this is a lengthy, cumbersome procedure, one which is less sensitive to the requirements of collective bargaining than the arbitration system.

Being able to arbitrate pension disputes is important. The company may argue that arbitration is unnecessary because pensions are regulated by the federal government; however, most pension disputes do not concern ERISA minimum pension standards but rather the intent of the negotiated pension agreement.

Arbitration is a superior mechanism for solving these kinds of disputes. For one thing, in arbitration the union presents the individual's case against the employer; under federal procedures the individual participant takes on the employer. That's a very important difference. It should be noted as well that the typical grievance procedure is not well designed for pension disputes. (Just imagine the look on a foreman's face while you're at the first step explaining a grievance over a particular pension claim.) To that end, most contracts that call for arbitration of pension disputes provide for a special procedure which eliminates the lower steps of the grievance procedure and involves the employer representative who has the authority to resolve pension disputes.

Joint Administrative Committees

Some local unions have gone considerably further than arbitration of disputes by negotiating joint administrative committees. The responsibility and authority of these joint committees vary from helping with claims (making sure a retiree has the right forms to fill out and understands the various retirement options) to having the responsibility and authority to determine the intent of the plan, and to determining, in a limited sense, "correct" benefit figures.

Joint committees have two main advantages. First, the individual participant can get assistance from the union's joint committee representatives in understanding benefit decisions. The representatives have the responsibility as well as the authority to make sure all its members receive the information they need to make good retirement decisions. The union joint committee representatives should not become financial advisors to the members, but rather watchdogs that make sure the members receive clear, concise information.

The second and possibly more important advantage (at least for collective bargaining purposes) is that the union pension committee can be a valuable resource for the union negotiator. If even one person on the bargaining committee is familiar with the pension plan because of participation on the pension committee, the negotiator will have much greater access to good information about the plan's operation and any problem areas that have come up over the years.

Plan Funding and Investments

Plan funding refers to the timing of contributions and amount of money to be set aside to meet the financial obligations of a pension plan. It is unusual for a single-employer plan to have extensive provisions regarding funding or, for that matter, any language at all. The typical attitude has been that the company is responsible for paying benefits; how it meets that responsibility is its concern.

When unions do negotiate in this area, they usually contract with regard to either the timing of contributions or the administration of unfunded liabilities (how quickly the company must write off its liabilities). The importance of timing may be seen in the example of a contract that requires a company to make its contributions on the final day of the plan year. The law allows the company 270 days after the close of the plan year, but negotiating an earlier date gets the money into the fund sooner. The earlier the plan starts to receive income from the contribution, the more secure it will be.

The value of negotiating over unfunded liability is demonstrated by a contract that calls for amortization of liabilities at a pace faster than the ERISA requirement (25 years, for instance, rather than 30 years). This is a two-edged sword, of course; the shorter the amortization period is, the more expensive and difficult it is to negotiate benefit improvements.

An important concern in the whole funding area is the issue of applications for funding waivers In order to keep the tax qualification of pension contributions, a company has to adhere to certain minimum and maximum funding rules. The company cannot simply make random yearly decisions about how much to put aside. However, if a company is confronted with a severe financial problem, it can petition the Internal Revenue Service to be relieved of its obligation to fund the pension plan for a given year. If the IRS grants that petition, the plan cannot increase the benefits promised by the plan until the waived funding requirement is made up in full.

The union has no say in the procedure to grant a funding waiver, and it has happened that a company has received a funding waiver for a year in which a benefit increase was to go into effect. In such a case the company would inform the union that because of the outstanding funding waiver, the negotiated increase cannot go into effect. This situation can occur because there is a conflict between the National Labor Relations Act and ERISA regarding increases and waivers. Eventually this should be resolved by the courts, but in the meantime it is important to negotiate contracts that restrict a company's right to seek funding waivers. The language might say that the company may not seek a funding waiver without approval of the local union. At least then you can sit down and negotiate; if the waiver is necessary, you can go after payback provisions that allow you to negotiate on pensions during the next round of negotiations.

Some older defined-benefit agreements spell out the contribution the company must make to the pension plan. Arguments about whether these are defined-contribution or defined-benefit plans could be endless, but when there are no individual accounts and the pension promises a specific benefit, the law views these as defined-benefit plans regardless of whether the labor agreement calls for a specific cents-per-hour contribution.

This situation actually creates a defined-benefit pension with a minimum funding requirement specified in the contract. An interesting situation would arise where the contract calls for a \$.50 per hour contribution to an overfunded plan. Because the plan is overfunded, the \$.50 contribution might not be tax-deductible. Neither the company nor the union would be very happy about this set of circumstances. The plan is secure if the benefits are fully funded, so why contribute more into the program? This mutual unhappiness can, of course, be corrected through negotiation. One obvious solution would be to increase pension benefits so the plan is no longer overfunded; the $.50 would then qualify for normal tax status.

Another area largely undeveloped in union pension contracts concerns pension fund investment. Chapter 10 will deal extensively with this topic, which is being widely discussed in the pension bargaining field. In any event, it is difficult and possibly ill-advised to nail down a specific set of investment rules in a three-year labor contract. Investment markets that appear to have low risk today may become quite risky in a matter of months, as did the long-term bond market in the early 1980s. Contract language involving pension fund investment should be largely confined to procedural language; that is, procedures for coming up with investment guidelines rather than the guidelines themselves.

Plan Amendment

In most areas of contract negotiation, you can rest assured that the words you agreed to at the table will stay put for the term of the agreement. This is not to say you won't have fights over what those words mean, but at least they'll be the same words for some specified period of time. Unfortunately, this is not true for pensions.

In order for company contributions to a pension plan to be deductible, they must have the blessing of the Internal Revenue Service, and the IRS changes its rules with a fair amount of regularity. In order to maintain the plan's qualification, pension language must be continuously modified. It neither makes sense to take the position that the company cannot change the language, nor to allow it to make wholesale changes without involving the bargaining committee. The most sensible approach is to negotiate language that allows the company to make modifications which are not inconsistent with the negotiated benefits (that is, to make friendly amendments), with the provision that all anticipated plan amendments be submitted to the bargaining committee for approval.

One practical problem with what are commonly called "ERISAfications" (changes in a pension plan to bring it into line with amendments to ERISA) is that it is frequently hard to tell whether a change is mandated under the law or whether the company is after a particularly convenient change. Since you probably don't read IRS or Department of Labor rulings on a daily basis, this can cause problems. When a situation arises, the easiest way to approach it is to ask the company for the name, address, and telephone number of the IRS or DOL officer with whom the company has been dealing. Talk directly to that person.

A pension plan's termination provisions are usually included in the "Plan Amendment" part of the contract; this aspect of pension plan language is covered in Chapter 11.

[*Author's Comment*—A company told me a few years ago that in order to be eligible for a funding waiver from the IRS it had to freeze benefit levels and benefit accrual. The union and I didn't question the need for the funding waiver; however, it seemed unreasonable that the IRS would demand a freeze on benefit accruals in addition to the freeze in benefit levels. We demanded, and got, the telephone number of the IRS officer and—surely enough—the officer's actual position had been that the IRS would look more favorably on the company's application for a waiver if the benefit accrual were to be frozen. This was hardly the position that the company presented at the table!

The moral is: make sure you take the time to double-check all company claims that "such and such is required by law."—J. MacD.]

Union Rights

In addition to an individual participant's rights, a number of specific union rights need to be negotiated for you to properly represent your members in the pension area.

The first is the union's right to regular information. Granted, there are informational rights under the NLRA and ERISA that are obtainable if you push hard enough. But it is much simpler to have a clause right in the labor agreement that specifies that the company is to provide the union with the following:

- The latest actuarial report as soon as it is available
- The annual DOL 5500 submission
- The annual trustees' report
- An annual listing of all active participants categorized by age, date of hire, vesting service, and benefit service
- A list of retirements during the previous year by type and amount of pension

Some local contracts go further, specifying that there will be "an annual meeting with the plan administrator, actuary, and trustee to review and answer any questions concerning the various reports." Such a provision gives the local union a chance to obtain a better understanding of the operation of the pension plan as well as a first-class education in the funding and investment aspects of a pension plan. This, of course, promotes more sophisticated bargaining.

The annual listing of all active participants categorized by age, date of hire, vesting service, and benefit service is important for discovering problems and errors in the administration of the plan. Mistakes that occur in record keeping are easier to correct shortly after they occur than 20 years later when the worker in question retires.

Further rights to negotiate for include the following:

- The union's right to help members with their pension applications, including paid time for reviewing applications
- The right to file grievances and to arbitrate disputes over the plan
- The right to notification of the company's intent to petition for a funding waiver
- The right to notification of the company's intent to submit a notice of intent to terminate the plan, with the right to negotiate regarding the timing of this submission

---

Table 6–4. Pension Plan Language Checklist

---

1. Participation	5. Benefit eligibility
2. Service accrual for:	6. Plan administration
a. Benefit calculation	7. Plan funding and investments
b. Benefit eligibility	8. Plan termination and
3. Break-in-Service rules	modification
4. Vesting rules	9. Union rights

7

Preparing to Bargain

Preparing to bargain in the pension area is similar to preparing to negotiate on other issues; the difference is that for pension bargaining, the negotiator requires even more information to do a thorough job. In this chapter, you will be learning where to find this information and how it applies to pension bargaining.

In general, the information falls into three categories: information internal to the local union and to the labor movement, information the company has, and information the negotiator will have to look for outside the union and the company.

Information the Union Already Has

Qualified Pension Plan

It's difficult to decide where you want to go with your pension if you don't know where you are right now. Therefore, first examine your pension contract. This may be more difficult than it seems, because you may never have seen the actual document. As mentioned in Chapter 2, the summary plan description, which by law must be distributed to all participants, is commonly thought to be the pension contract. It isn't.

The document you need is the qualified pension plan ("qualified" meaning that the contract has been approved by the Internal Revenue Service for purposes of tax qualification, which allows the company to deduct its contributions to the plan). There are probably only a few copies of this document, so don't be surprised if the company does not have one readily available.

Amendments to the Qualified Pension Plan

In addition to locating the main document, you have to make sure you have all its amendments. Pension plans are amended or re-written with some regularity, more often than most labor agreements. This is because the IRS often updates its regulations about what has to be in a pension contract for it to be tax-qualified. Check with the plan administrator to see if you have the most current version of the pension agreement; the summary plan description will note the administrator for your particular agreement.

Once you've found your qualified plan and all its amendments, set aside some time to read it. Pension agreements are designed to comply with IRS regulations, not to be understandable to the general public. Don't let this discourage you. If there are sections you don't understand (and there will be—probably only the person who wrote it understands it fully), make a note about it. Early in negotiations, review those sections with the company's benefits representative.

Because qualified pension plans are too complex to use effectively at the bargaining table, develop a summary of the plan that includes important elements of its key sections. Appendix G shows a form that bargaining committees can use to summarize their pension plans. The form has space for a summary of each major area of the plan, with additional space for comments. This kind of form can be particularly helpful to the full-time union representative or business agent responsible for servicing a group of locals, especially when a number of negotiations are going on at the same time.

Previous Contract Negotiations

Two other sources of help available to the local are the initial proposals submitted during the most recent pension bargaining negotiations and the final settlement agreement. The initial proposals will demonstrate the kind of problems the local was trying to solve the last time around, and the agreement will show if it made any progress. This is important because good pensions don't spring up overnight. They are usually the result of consistent small gains over a period of time. You have to look at the picture almost from the beginning in order to identify these small gains.

For example: the committee's ultimate goal is to eliminate the actuarial reduction for those who retire after age 62. Because there were more immediate problems during the last negotiation, the committee was successful only in cutting the actuarial reduction to 3 percent a year between ages 62 and 65. Now that three years have gone by, the original chair of the bargaining committee has moved on to the financial secretary's job, and most of the other committee members are new, too. If no one reviews the proposals put forth three years ago, the committee will probably miss an opportunity to improve the plan.

This should tell you something about when to start preparing for the next round of negotiations: as soon as the current settlement is ratified. At that point, make some notes about what the bargaining committee tried to accomplish, where it made improvements, where it was not able to get any improvements, and the specific reasons. Because most agreements are for three years, you are not likely to remember all the details from one negotiation to the next. Even if you have a good memory, you might not be around; it's not unusual to find substantial changes in leadership and staff between contracts. Do a favor for the people who come after you—write down your observations.

Another source of information (of mixed value for pension negotiations although vital for other aspects of the union contract) is feedback from the members. They are usually familiar with contract language involving daily concerns such as holiday pay and job posting. But workers retire only once, and like severance pay, retirement is one benefit they do not experience on a regular basis. Because the members do not have the opportunity to learn how it operates, their comments on the pension tend to be unspecific and fairly uninformed.

One solution is to establish a union pension committee. This committee can handle questions concerning retirement issues and help members file for their pensions. Members who serve on these committees usually become quite expert at understanding the plan, its operation, and its problems. At contract time, having a pension committee member available can save a lot of time and energy.

Information Available Through the Company

Much of the information needed for pension negotiations is available only through the company. How do you get it? You request it in a letter, sent by certified mail in case of future problems. A copy of such a letter is reproduced as Appendix H.

Does the company really have to provide all this information? If it's the first time you've sent this kind of request to the company, management will be asking the same question. Don't worry; the company will come around, because the law requires it to provide this information. Although no specific law says that it must provide each item listed in the sample letter, the National Labor Relations Act of 1935 requires the company "to bargain with the recognized union in 'good faith' " over wages, hours, and other conditions of employment. As mentioned in Chapter 2, the NLRB has ruled that pensions are included in "wages, hours, and other conditions of employment." The Board also has ruled that "good faith" bargaining includes providing the union with that information it needs to bargain intelligently. If the company refuses to provide the information, it is probably bargaining in bad faith, and you should consider filing an unfair labor practice charge.

Make your request early so that the company has time to collect the information. If it is a small company, it may take a considerable amount of time, and if the company is part of a larger corporation, the information may have to come from headquarters. Another reason to start early is to allow time to persuade the company should it prove hesitant to deliver the information.

When the requested material finally arrives, you're probably going to wonder if it is all necessary. Right now, it probably is not, but remember that a pension is a benefit which develops *over time*. It's important to have on hand an information base for making comparisons from year to year. Each item asked for in the letter in Appendix H will be helpful to the committee at some point, perhaps not in this round of negotiations, but surely at some future date.

For example, when the local goes into negotiations three years from now, the committee will discover that the average age of pension plan participants has dropped from 45 to 35. That's because the plating business has picked up. The company has landed a small defense contract and hired a couple of dozen new people. When the bargaining committee checks the figures, it will note that the average length of service has fallen, too. If the committee members are alert, they'll see that the cents-per-hour cost for $1 worth of monthly benefits will be less than it was over the last contract. That information will be very helpful to the committee in its discussions with management.

Beyond the usefulness of the information, Local 3520's letter communicates something important to management: that the local union is very serious about the pension program and its improvement. It's like the old joke about hitting the donkey on the head with a two-by-four: it doesn't make the animal go any faster, but it certainly focuses its attention. The letter is the first whack, you might say—the attention-getter.

What the Information Means

The following discussion will explain what the information gathered from the company means and how the committee can use it.

Data on Active Pension Plan Participants

Information about the age and benefit service of active pension plan participants is essential if the bargaining committee plans to make any rough estimates of benefit costs. At a minimum it will provide an idea about the direction of pension costs. An aging work force, for instance, means increased costs over the years; a younger work force means lower costs. In the economic climate of the early 1980s, widespread unemployment meant the average age and service statistic was likely to take a dramatic jump upward, with a corresponding jump in pension costs.

Although such increases are not the sort of thing you would bring up in negotiations, it's best to be aware of the facts. When management finds the bad news, you can bet it will make the most of it. Prepare a strategy for responding. This might be the time to mend your nets and go for cost-free or low-cost benefits that improve security. Build membership support for the pension improvements to strengthen your hand with the company. Check to see if the actuarial assumptions are realistic. Some of these strategies might not work, but others might. You have nothing to lose by thinking of alternative strategies in the face of bad news.

Additionally, having data on all three types of service— seniority, vesting, and benefit—will help determine whether there are problems in the way service is counted. Most service-counting rules are understandable; their effects may not be so obvious. For example: the bargaining committee reviews the service statistics and notes that the members' benefit service is almost always substantially less than either their seniority or vesting service. This indicates either that the hours rule is too high, that the way hours are counted misses a lot of time, or that there was a year or years in which most of the members were on an extensive layoff that caused a loss of benefit service. Checking service records will bring the problem to light and provide time to think about a solution.

Data on Retired Participants

Information about retired participants broken into date of retirement, age, credited service, and amount of the monthly benefit is especially important if you have a complex benefit formula involving Social Security cutoffs, percentage of earnings applied to different time periods and different amounts, and other factors. You can read these in the pension document and still have no idea what a typical worker is going to retire with; there are simply too many variables. Calculating an average monthly benefit by age and type of benefit payment option will provide a clear picture of what level of benefit your formula provides.

These figures may also be used to calculate the average age of retirement and the percentage of membership that retires early. If you discover that the average age of retirement is moving up, be aware that this means the cost is coming down. Further, companies usually talk about the worst-case scenario when discussing early retirement benefit improvements, moaning that everybody will retire early to use the new benefit. That's not likely. To counter company arguments, it's helpful to have a good idea how many workers might use the benefit. Average age of retirement statistics will suggest the answers.

Using the age at retirement and monthly benefit averages, it is usually possible to figure out how the company's actuaries calculate the early-retirement deduction. They may be reducing by a percentage multiplied by the number of years before age 65, or compounding down from age 65, which is the method most advantageous to the early retiree (see "Actuarial Reduction," in Chapter 5).

Annual Company Contributions Schedule and Level of Contributions

Knowing the company's annual contribution to the plan enables the committee to calculate past pension costs in terms of cents-per-hour. With the trend toward rising interest rates, pension costs frequently fall, at least in industries that have been able to maintain a stable work force. Such a development naturally gives support to union demands for increased pension benefits.

Federal pension laws give considerable latitude as to when pension plan contributions must be made. A company is allowed to make its annual contribution to the plan up to seven months after the close of the plan year. The date a company actually makes its contribution is important, because the longer a company defers its contribution, the less time it will have to earn interest and the higher the eventual cost of the pension program.

The Three Most Recent Actuarial Evaluations

An actuarial evaluation is the report from the actuary to the company concerning the financial status of the plan. Each report contains a statement of assets and a detailed account of plan liabilities and their source. These reports vary considerably in readability, organization of information, and type of detail provided. Further, if your plan has fewer than 100 participants, ERISA requires a report only once every three years. However, it's possible to negotiate more frequent reports.

Each actuarial report also contains an estimate of unfunded liability, which is important if the plan terminates as of a given date (in the event of a plant closing, for example). Further, the actuarial report recommends a range of contributions based on plan provisions, the demographics of the participants, and the actuarial assumptions; the range includes the maximum contribution for which the company can claim tax deductions, the minimum under current ERISA regulations, and usually one which the actuary recommends, which typically falls somewhere between the maximum and minimum. This information will provide an idea of the possible range of plan costs.

It's difficult to quarrel with an actuary's arithmetic, but if you have a problem with the report, question the assumptions used. The details of the assumptions (Appendix I) are found in each report, usually on a page toward the back. By comparing the three most recent reports it can be determined if the actuary has changed any of the assumptions. If the retirement age shows a pattern of increases—from age 65 to age 66.5, for example—the pension will be correspondingly less expensive.

The Three Latest Department of Labor 5500 Forms

The Department of Labor 5500 form (Appendix J) is the financial document that ERISA requires a company to submit each year.

Information on these forms tends to be somewhat outdated because the filing requirements give companies quite a while to submit them, and there is little follow-up to see that companies actually do submit them. Once you have the form in front of you, use the worksheet (Appendix K) to set up the information from the DOL 5500 in systematic order. Much of the information also shows up in other material that the bargaining committee is requesting, but the DOL 5500 is a handy check against other figures and has the information all in one place.

The Three Latest Trustee Reports

Trustee reports provide information about the investment performance of the funds; the asset managers send them to the company. The reports will itemize contributions from the company, payments to beneficiaries, and earnings from investments. Trustee reports vary considerably in quality and, unfortunately, the trustee of record may be only a conduit for the money between the company and professional money managers. The trustee of record's report is often merely an accounting statement. The two sets of facts you want from the report are the annual fund earnings and details about where the money is invested.

If the fund consistently earns more than the actuary's assumption, the cost of the pension program will be lower than estimated; if the earnings are lower than the estimate, the cost will be higher. This is important information for the negotiating team to know. (The issue of pension fund investment will be discussed more fully in Chapter 10.)

Further, as mentioned before, one of the major goals of a pension is benefit security. Asset managers have a disturbing tendency to believe in the stock market as an article of faith; they always talk about the long-run performance of the market. This assumption is questionable on its face, but more importantly, companies fail not in the long run but in the short run. It's important that pension assets be invested with an eye to low risk. The trustee report will give you an idea about the risk exposure of your members' pension money.

Information from Outside Sources

As with many issues of national, economic, and social significance, there is almost too much information available about pensions Keeping up on all aspects of the subject is an impossible task, but there are certain sources of information outside the company and outside union circles that can help the pension negotiator both in developing sound approaches to pension problems and in actual negotiations.

Basic Retirement Benefits

It's a rare negotiation in which the bargaining committee fails to submit a proposal to improve the basic pension formula, and it's the rare company that doesn't want to know what's wrong with the current benefit. The basic answer, from the committee's standpoint, is, "The members want an improvement. We won't get a ratification without one." If you don't have that kind of backing, facts and figures won't help you. But even when you can argue quite accurately that pensions are high among your members' priorities, you will still need other information to convince the company that this desire comes out of a perceived need. The first place to start looking for this information is in your own community.

For instance, what do other workers in your area get in the way of pension benefits? Most local unions are listed in the Yellow Pages under the heading "Labor Organizations." Start calling. In addition, the AFL-CIO city or county central labor body will have a listing of its local affiliates that includes names and phone numbers of local union officers. (If your local union is not yet affiliated with the central body, become affiliated. It's a lot easier to get good information if you know the leadership of other local unions.)

After comparing pension benefits in the area, you'll probably want to investigate whether your company is sponsoring any other pension plans. If so, what benefits do locals in the other divisions earn? The National Labor Relations Board publishes a listing of organized plants; the listing is arranged by company name and by international union. Once you have the locations of other subsidiaries and the unions involved, getting the desired information is simply a matter of phoning the respective international unions. For unorganized plants, you can request the company's DOL 5500s for the facility from the Department of Labor.

Pension Language

The next question the committee faces is language. You know what the problem is, but what words do you use to solve it? Although it is risky to pull language verbatim from other contracts, it is often helpful to look at how other plans have approached certain problems. A number of reporting services provide information on model contracts and short summaries of various pension topics. A list of the major reporting services appears under "Pension Reporting Services" below. Subscriptions to these publications are fairly expensive for a local union or an international representative, but they are not too expensive for most public libraries. If the library is reluctant to subscribe, it may be possible to change the staff's mind if enough of your members and other local unions complain. The negotiating skills you use with your company should be helpful in dealing with this situation, too.

Pension Reporting Services

There are two general labor reporting services available:

Daily Labor Report, Bureau of National Affairs, Inc., 1231 25th Street, N.W., Washington, D.C. 20037

This daily reporter covers all aspects of labor relations, and is a good way to keep up with current events in the pension area. More important are its regularly updated indexes, which allow up-to-date research on pension topics. This publication also is a good source for summaries of major agreements.

Collective Bargaining Negotiations and Contracts (also a Bureau of National Affairs, Inc., publication)

This is a two-volume binder, regularly updated, which has both general information for negotiators and a section on pensions that includes short reports on basic trends.

The following three services deal specifically with pensions. Each has advantages and disadvantages in terms of indexing, readability, format, and so forth.

BNA Pension Reporter (also a Bureau of National Affairs, Inc., service, see above address)

Pension Plan Guide, Commerce Clearing House, 4025 West Peterson Avenue, Chicago, Ill. 60646

EBPR Research Reports, Charles D. Spencer & Associates, Inc., 222 West Adams Street, Chicago, Ill. 60606

For information regarding issues surrounding pension investment topics, *Labor & Investments*, published by the AFL-CIO's Industrial Union Department, is a helpful monthly publication. (It's available, free of charge, to members of IUD-affiliated unions. A subscription for others costs $70 annually.) Also helpful is *Pension and Investment Age*, published by Crain Communications, Inc. (Write to *Pension and Investment Age*, Circulation Department, 740 Rush Street, Chicago, Ill. 60611. The cost is $52 annually.)

Some veteran business agents may say that you don't need all this fancy stuff to get the pension you want. Just tell the company what you want and, if you don't get it, strike. While that certainly communicates clearly to the company on one level, such grand gestures miss the point that power depends on the type of information available. The strongest raw economic power in the world—the power to withhold your labor—is worthless if you don't have the information to guide the effective use of this power. This is never more true than in the area of pension bargaining. The opportunities must be seen before they can be exploited.

8

Pension Bargaining Timeline

For several chapters pensions have been discussed as if they were a separate negotiation. In fact, there are only limited situations in which it makes sense to talk about a pension negotiation per se, such as when the expiration dates of the pension agreement and the labor contract are not the same, or during a transfer of ownership that includes a rollover of pension assets and liabilities and the desire to start anew. These situations are rare. Ordinarily, the pension agreement expires with the contract, with the result that the pension is only one of many items on the negotiating agenda. And, as management is likely to point out, it is all funded from the same source and that source has its limits.

Therefore, every contract negotiation starts with two unknowns: how much money is available and how to best distribute that money. Finding the answers to both is a complex process that prevents settling in any major area until you have a rough estimate of both. Management and union bargaining committees alike arrive at their estimates of the other's limits during the give-and-take of early sessions. The communication is indirect but clear to those who know how to read the signals.

The importance of understanding the limits and allocations is illustrated dramatically by the experience of a young international union staffer known to the authors. During his first contract negotiation, he was sent to a large local as the international's expert to negotiate the pension part of the contract. He arrived at the table convinced beyond a doubt that, because he had justice on his side, he would make believers of everybody.

The result was a disaster. The problem was that he was negotiating a set of pension proposals in a vacuum, unaware that the company team had judged that there needed to be a wage increase to get a contract ratification. If the company moved on the pension proposals, there wouldn't be enough left for the wage increase.

However, the international's hotshot had created enough of an uproar about pensions that the company believed pension improvements were a key issue to the membership. With these two needs in conflict, the company negotiators judged that no matter how they moved there would be a strike. Rather than admit now just how much money was available, they decided to take the strike and discuss the money only after the workers had been on the street for a while, when priorities would be a little clearer. The strike was eventually settled with a substantial wage increase and no pension increase.

Unfortunately, there really was a serious pension problem at this location. After months of hard work at the bargaining table, the union had accomplished nothing in the pension area, not even a small gain.

In order to bargain effectively in the pension area, you have to understand not only pension plan design, but also the collective bargaining process. You can't negotiate pensions in a vacuum; you must be sensitive to and aware of the total bargaining agenda.

While it is beyond the scope of this book to discuss negotiating techniques in depth, this chapter will discuss the bargaining process as it relates to pensions.

Choosing and Preparing Proposals

Most local unions have a way to identify priority issues and proposals for an upcoming round of negotiations. This may vary in formality from fairly extensive surveys to just talking around the plant. However, these processes often don't work for pensions, because they are unlikely to identify obscure, but important issues, such as "crediting all time on layoff for the period 1962 to 1964." Even if there is sizable support for improving the retirement program, the support frequently will be no more specific than "we want to improve our pension plan." Rarely will there be a suggestion to improve it by a specific amount. This gives the bargaining committee considerable latitude in developing proposals, but it also makes more work for it.

Although preparations for bargaining were covered earlier in Chapter 7, a few comments are appropriate here with regard to drafting an initial proposal and selecting issues.

Define Problems

Start by identifying the problems rather than trying to come up with specific proposals for solutions. When starting from a proposal rather than a problem, the tendency is to lock in your thinking to one solution which, after a while, becomes the only possible solution rather than one of many possible solutions. In pensions, as with most things, there is more than one way to achieve a goal.

For example, some plans have caps on service accrual, providing x dollars a month per year of credited service with a maximum of 30 years' service. There's obviously an equity problem here in that one group of workers (those with over 30 years' service) is not accumulating any pension credit for a year of work while others are. While the best solution might be to remove the cap and allow for unlimited credit for service, it isn't the only one. You could also negotiate yearly actuarial improvements for those with 30 years or more, COLA improvements while those workers are actively employed, or a special retiree medical insurance program for people with over 30 years of service. Remember, your basic problem is not eliminating the cap, but helping the members who have 30 or more years of service; if you can't accomplish this one way, look for another way to address the issue.

Submit Alternatives

Sometimes it makes sense initially to submit several proposals regarding the same problem. This allows for flexibility in future discussions. There are drawbacks, however. For starters, the company negotiators are likely to be taken aback when they see all your proposals the first time. In order to smooth the progress of negotiations, be sure to explain that each proposal responds to the same basic problem and, while you don't expect to get all of what you've proposed, you do expect the problem to be seriously considered. Point out that the various proposals represent your best thinking about alternatives and directions the negotiations might take.

However, avoid this shotgun approach if you want a specific solution and if you have the bargaining power and membership support to get it.

Include Minor Issues

Always try to include some small items that are not overly expensive and do not involve fundamental policy, so that you can make some improvements, however small, every contract. It's demoralizing when negotiations come down to the wire and you have nothing on the table except major cost and policy issues.

Put It in Writing

All proposals should be in writing, but don't be overly concerned about nailing down every detail. Keep your proposals short and clear. Areas of ambiguity or confusion can be cleared up by your chief spokesperson during the initial submission. Your first concern is to get agreement that there is a problem; your second, to get agreement, at least in principle, on direction. You can work on the details later in the negotiation.

Document the Problem

Information supporting the existence of the problem and its causes is more important than the specifics of the proposal. Few situations are more embarrassing than to have a company negotiator ask you why you're concerned about something when all you can respond is "because." You need to be able to describe the problem by citing specific examples.

Review Past Negotiations

Finally, in drafting proposals be sure to go back to the previous negotiation to find out what proposals were submitted when, where the committee was able to make improvements, and where it ran into opposition.

Once you've completed evaluating the plan and targeted its major problems, you won't have to worry about those problems changing significantly for quite a while. A good pension is built piece by piece over many different negotiations.

The First Day of Bargaining

Housekeeping chores usually occupy most of the first bargaining day's agenda, including details such as where the meetings will take place, what the timetable is, and what arrangements will be made for reimbursing the bargaining committee for lost time. Initial proposals may be exchanged, but little real bargaining will take place. It is always a good idea to make an economics proposal on the first day, or at least early in the negotiations. This is especially important in the pension area because you want the company to be thinking about solutions to the major problems. In order to get the company thinking in this direction, you have to state your view of the problems.

Further, unlike a wage increase or an additional holiday, a pension change requires the company to hire an outsider—the actuary—to evaluate the potential cost impact. This can take a lot of time, so submit pension proposals early to give the company a chance to consult its experts.

How to Highlight Pensions

If the bargaining committee makes its economics proposal early in the contract talks, it is still faced with the problem of separating pensions from the rest of the package. It's one thing to tell management that pensions are a high priority, but remember that just about every proposal you submit is a priority for someone in your bargaining unit. The shift worker sees the shift bonus as a top priority; the skilled tradespeople see skilled trades equity as a top priority; younger members with families see a general wage increase as the major issue. Although everyone on the committee is bargaining with the general welfare of the membership in mind, it's naive to assume that there will be agreement about what "improving the general welfare" means this early in the talks. Without further information it's too early to make choices, but it's important to get the company thinking about the pension plan.

This can be done many ways. You've already told the company that pensions are important by asking for information about the plan. The order in which you submit your economic proposals also sends a message to the company; if you group your pension proposals with other obviously important issues, you communicate that pensions are a big issue. On the other hand, if you group pensions with housekeeping proposals, you give the company a very different message.

Allocating Time

Further, the amount of time spent on an issue indicates its importance. If, for example, you spend an hour on the need for a new dental program, but merely hand the company the pension proposals without comment, you've communicated that the dental proposal is more important. On the other hand, if you spend half an hour on all other economic proposals combined, and proceed to discuss pensions for the next four hours, you've certainly given the company a different clue.

Time allocation is one of the more interesting aspects of pension bargaining. If you take the more common economic issues—a general wage increase or a holiday, for instance—it's difficult to think of anything to say other than "we want it," regardless of an issue's importance. Even with a fair amount of research on area industries or national trends, it's difficult to wax eloquent for more than 15 minutes.

This isn't the case with pensions, however. It's easy to use up days, if that's the committee's strategy, talking about pensions. Before negotiations begin, the bargaining committee will have over 100 pages of documents to review concerning the operation of the plan, including, among others, the qualified plan document, several actuarial reports, and the DOL 5500 forms. That first day the committee may have pages of questions about how the plan works in terms of language and funding. Discussion of these questions has two main functions. First, it shows the company that you actually read all the information you asked for. Second, the discussion further educates the bargaining committee about the plan's operation. Because few people will be interested in something they don't understand, time spent educating the committee, regardless of the forum, is time well spent.

At the end of the first session it's inevitable that the membership will confront the committee to find out what was discussed. If pensions occupied a substantial amount of time, that fact will be all over the plant by the next day, and will help the committee to stimulate support for pension improvements.

In order to allow for substantive discussion on the first day, it is important to notify the company that the committee intends to discuss the operation of the pension plan. This encourages the company to send someone to the table who at least understands the questions. Using the first day of negotiations not only to submit proposals but to review the operation of the plan will force this company negotiator to think more specifically about the pension and to interact with the company's pension experts. If the committee is well prepared, there will almost always be questions the company team can't respond to without further investigation. This keeps the pension discussions open with the need to return to them at a later date.

Should the company bring its pension experts to the table, this can be a plus or a minus. Sometimes these people can talk at length about the virtues of the current plan, and if they sound convincing enough they can take some of the starch out of the bargaining committee. If it looks as if this will be a danger, make sure the union negotiator keeps control of the meeting and that the meeting serves its intended purpose: answering the specific questions prepared by the bargaining committee.

If the committee handles things correctly, by the end of the first day the company should know beyond a shadow of a doubt both that pensions are a priority and what problems the union wants addressed in current talks.

Language Sessions

In the typical negotiation, the bulk of bargaining time is spent on contract language issues, because the problems and solutions are complex. Typically, pensions are hardly mentioned during this discussion, giving the union negotiators a chance to promote pension issues among the membership. Remember that the company does not rely exclusively on the position of the bargaining committee in making its estimate of what's important to the workers. The company gets constant feedback from its own people about what is important to the workers. Make sure management hears the same message from your members that it hears from you across the table. The time during which language is the major focus of negotiations can be used very effectively to orchestrate this situation.

This is also the time to explore carefully different solutions to any complex pension problems. A company rarely will commit itself to specifics during this early part of bargaining, but frequently it is possible to get an idea of the direction in which the company might go. If an agreement on direction can be reached during the language discussion, potentially harmful false starts will be avoided.

Many pension proposals will deal with what are primarily language issues: the union's contractual right to see the various pension documents, a modification of the definition of an hour, and so on. A company typically will try to defer these matters until the discussion of economics, on the grounds that anything regarding the pension plan is to be considered an economics issue.

You don't have to agree with this rather arbitrary classification of issues, but your response should be a strategic decision based upon the situation. You may agree with the company, you may hold your proposal on the table until the bitter end of the language discussions, or you may refuse to move on to economics until the issue is settled. You can only decide specific strategy when actually at the table; the important thing is not to let pension language issues get lost in the shuffle during the final, frantic days of negotiation. If you agree to shift some pension language proposals to economics, make sure it is clear to the company that you are not withdrawing them but simply deferring discussion to a more appropriate time.

First Session on Economics

After the committee has reached tentative agreement with the company on language issues, the first session devoted to economics is similar to the first day. Very little actual negotiation occurs, but the atmosphere is charged. If a complete economics proposal has been submitted previously, this is when the company makes its initial response; otherwise the union can use this session to complete its proposal. Regardless, at this meeting the committee should highlight the union's concern for pension problems and should reintroduce any issues that were shifted out of language discussions.

Even in good times a company's initial proposal usually is sparse. The management team will have a rough idea of the amount it is allowed to spend, but it's still too early to begin allocating the money. It is important at this point to press the company for its position on the various pension proposals. While this can be frustrating, you may get important information about the company position. Is it simply a matter of money? Are corporate policy issues in the background? Are other negotiations under way in other plants that will have an impact on yours? Everything you can find out now may help later in the negotiations.

Early Counterproposals

When both the union and the company have made a few proposals and counterproposals, the pressure will begin to build to trim the union proposals so the parties can concentrate on the central economic issues. At this point the union frequently will not know whether the pension issues are going to be dealt with in a significant way. However, there will be considerable pressure to drop the smaller pension proposals, and it is to the union's advantage to resist this pressure. If the committee drops the proposal for contractually required pension reports to the union, for example, or for the small modification in the definition of hours, the company may not move on the major pension issues. Once you drop the smaller issues, you may be left with only two options at the end of negotiations: agree to the contract with no pension improvements, or strike. If there's no support for a strike, the committee will have done lots of work without achieving even marginal improvements.

Final Hours Before the Contract Expires

The final hours before the old contract expires are the most difficult stage of any negotiation. At this point the bargaining committee has to make a judgment call about whether an agreement is going to be reached or not. Sometimes the committee can almost taste a settlement or a strike, and it has to adjust its strategy accordingly.

If it's reasonably clear a settlement is going to be reached, this is the time to scramble for whatever small improvements you can get. Once the parties are so close that a settlement is likely, the company will know it too. Any significant improvements past this point are unlikely.

On the other hand, if it looks as if a strike is inevitable, it makes sense to keep as much on the table as possible. Don't give up all the small issues before calling the strike. It's unlikely that withdrawing a few small issues is going to bring a settlement if significant differences remain between the parties. Further, you'll limit your options. Although the bargaining rules don't apply once a strike is under way, in reality it's difficult to reintroduce a proposal without making a bad situation worse. Once a proposal is withdrawn, consider it lost.

During these final hours, pension modifications are rarely handled the way other proposals are. It's customary in nonpension areas to agree tentatively to the actual contract language changes, but with pensions this is rare. Any agreements are usually regarding what will be done after the signing of the contract rather than the actual language needed to accomplish that end.

For this reason it is important to walk through several examples involving actual members, so that there is a clear understanding of what has been agreed to.

To take a simple example, let's say you've agreed to a $.50 increase per month per year of credited service in the first and second years of a three-year agreement, plus the elimination of the actuarial reduction for the years between age 62 and 65 to become effective at the beginning of the third year. It may seem needless work, but before you reach agreement, discuss several examples of members in different situations. Take Bill G., who is currently on layoff and might not come back—if he exercises his option to retire, will he get the increase? What about Elaine M., who could retire in the third year of the contract when she's 60? Together with the company, walk though the calculation of her reduction so that everybody understands the procedure. There are some situations where the issues are sufficiently complex that the committee and company should sign the examples of the calculations to make sure that when the language is drafted to accomplish these results, there is no confusion about what you want to achieve.

Ratification Meeting and After

To discuss ratification meetings in detail is beyond the scope of this book. Briefly, the central purpose of a ratification meeting is for the membership to decide whether to accept a settlement and continue to work, or to reject it and strike. For the process to work well, it's important that the membership be well-informed about what has and has not been accomplished. In most areas this is a fairly easy task; after all, it's hard to confuse people over the details of a $.50 an hour wage increase.

Pension improvements are another matter. Before the ratification meeting it's worth your time and effort to decide how the pension modifications will be presented, who will present them, and what examples will be used to illustrate the changes. There's nothing more difficult than trying to develop a good example off the top of your head to clarify the confusion that is being loudly demonstrated by the 500 members on the floor. Take time to plan!

Now that you're finally ratified, you've almost earned a rest— but not just yet. When the modified pension plan is finally ready to be printed, you still have to proofread and check it to make sure everything you agreed to has been addressed.

Make sure, too, that when the negotiation is complete you take the time to jot down a few notes about what the committee tried to accomplish, what it succeeded in getting, and, most importantly, what it left unfinished. It's never too early to start planning for the next round of talks. Make copies of your notes so that at least one set is available for the next bargaining committee to use.

9

Pension Bargaining and Costs

When the parties begin a contract negotiation, they work within a set of limits. The company has an estimate of how much money it's willing to commit during any round of negotiations, and the union has an estimate of the improvements in wages, benefits, and working conditions it needs to get a ratification. Although neither party knows for sure what the final limits are until they have been achieved, both sides continue to make calculated guesses along the way. These rough limits are important in that the relative and absolute costs of improving any particular fringe benefit will have an impact on what can be accomplished in other areas.

For example, consider health insurance. Because of the dramatic rise in health care costs over the past several years, health insurance premiums have increased; correspondingly, each increase lessens your ability at the bargaining table to improve wages or increase vacation time. The exact relationship between maintaining a given health insurance program and forgoing other wage or benefit improvements is rarely made explicit by an employer telling the bargaining committee, "the cost of the health insurance plan has gone up 10 cents per hour worked; therefore, we propose a wage increase of $.55 rather than the $.65 we originally planned." Even when this does happen, you can never be sure whether it is a genuine tradeoff or a bargaining ploy. In any event, an improvement in one area clearly has a cost in terms of what can be accomplished in another area. Therefore, it's important to be able to make rough estimates of the costs associated with a given economic proposal.

This chapter, then, will show how to calculate the cents-per-hour cost of an existing pension plan so that you will be able to determine and track cost trends over an extended period of time. You'll learn a simple method of calculating the costs of basic benefit improvements, and examine the implications of pension costs for various bargaining strategies.

A comprehensive introduction to the basics of contract and settlement costing techniques is beyond the scope of this book; however, Appendix L provides a general introduction to costing for several fringe benefits, including insurance, holidays, and vacation. The basics also can be learned through labor education programs.

Determining the Cost of Current Benefits

Two weeks from now you're going to be sitting down with the plant manager and the industrial relations chief from XYZ Corporation to open negotiations. One of the union's bargaining priorities this time is to improve the pension plan. As part of your preparations, you've already sent the company a letter requesting information you need to bargain intelligently (see Appendix H), including information on the annual employer contribution to the pension plan for the three previous years. The company's response indicated that its annual contributions to the pension plan were as follows:

Year 1	$1,200,000
Year 2	$ 890,000
Year 3	$ 950,000

Finding Cents-per-Hour Worked

You have to work with this raw data to transform it into something helpful. First, you want the cost in cents-per-hour worked, because most union members are paid by the hour. (In cases where employees are paid a yearly salary, the relevant figure would be the average cost per employee per year.) As indicated in Table 9–1, to find the cents-per-hour figure, divide the annual contribution first by the number of workers in the bargaining unit (which will give you the annual cost per worker) and then divide that figure by the average number of hours worked per year. The result will be the average cost in cents-per-hour worked.

Detecting Cost Trends

This series of cents-per-hour costs does not provide specific information on the cost of proposed improvements, but it can pro-

Table 9–1. Formula for Finding Cost of a Pension Plan in
Cents-per-Hour Worked

Year	Annual Contribution ÷	Number of Employees =	Average Cost per Employee per Year ÷	Average Hours Worked per Year =	Cents per Hour
1	$1,200,000	1,000	$1,200.00	2,000	$.60
2	890,000	950	936.84	1,900	.49
3	950,000	900	1,055.56	1,800	.59

vide important information on cost trends. For example, here are two cases where such trends do provide the negotiator with some important information.

Employer A has the following cents-per-hour pension costs.

Year 1	$.37
Year 2	$.35
Year 3	$.23
Year 4	$.14

As you can see, Employer A contributed less and less on a cents-per-hour basis over a period of four years. The causes of this cost decline were complex. There was a steady increase in employment over the four-year period, which caused a drop in the average age and service of the participants. Employees contributed 2.5 percent of their gross income to the fund and, because the retirement benefit was based on a career-average formula, employee contributions rose at the same rate as current wages. Benefits, however, increased much more slowly because they were based on lifetime earnings. Finally, the fund's investments did so well that the actuary raised the interest rate assumption to 6 percent from 5 percent. All these factors caused a severe drop in the employer's cents-per-hour cost over the four-year period.

Just by looking at the decreasing costs to the employer you can see that now is a good time to negotiate pension improvements. While you shouldn't expect the employer to simply accept any proposal you make, you have the advantage of a much younger work force and good fund earnings, which lead to a higher interest rate assumption. Most of the trends are in your favor. During the previous contract talks the local was able to make progress toward eliminating employee contributions, and although the committee was not able to eliminate the career-average formula, it was able to establish a minimum benefit formula of $10 per month per year of credited service, which will help a large percentage of members at this location. Other factors also enabled the bargaining committee to make these improvements, but knowing what happened to costs over the previous three years didn't hurt.

Then, of course, there's the other side of the coin. Employer B's cents-per-hour costs were:

Year 1	$1.10
Year 2	$1.00
Year 3	$1.25
Year 4	$1.40

Employer B is in the auto parts supply business, and while there was a brief reduction in pension costs from Year 1 to Year 2 because of investment experience and a modification in the actuarial assumption, the reduction was wiped out by a massive recession in the auto industry, which led to substantial layoffs. This caused a dramatic rise in the average age and seniority of the group. More importantly, most of the workers laid off were vested. Although they were not accumulating new pension benefits, the liability for their accumulated vested benefits didn't disappear. This fixed liability now had to be spread over fewer workers and fewer production hours.

No negotiator will be happy to see a cost stream like this one. However, you are better off knowing about a sudden cost increase than not. At least this knowledge gives you an idea of how difficult bargaining will be; it's not easy to negotiate significant pension improvements at a location where current costs have increased 30 to 40 percent. You will probably have to spend more time developing membership support for pension improvements in order to increase your power at the bargaining table. You may also want to work on areas of the pension that are less costly than a basic benefit improvement, such as improved annuity options, better disability, and better plan termination provisions. Still, knowing the dimensions of the problem, you can start working out bargaining strategies.

Interpreting Cost Data

You can keep track of cents-per-hour cost figures on the DOL 5500 analysis form provided in Appendix K. In the example at the beginning of the chapter, the calculation for XYZ Corporation was based on annual contribution figures provided by the employer; the same set of calculations could be done relying on the DOL 5500. Keep in mind, though, that DOL 5500s frequently are one or two years out of date; you may have to rely on employer figures for the most recent year.

Another aspect of interpreting cost data is determining what figure to use for the number of employees in the bargaining unit. If the work force is fairly stable, this isn't an issue, but if any dramatic changes occur during the year, you must allow for this. If, for example, there were 1,000 employees in the bargaining unit at the beginning of the plan year, but because of layoffs there were only 500 at the end, averaging will be necessary. Failure to average would result in cost estimates which would be too high or too low. Since the average number of employees is 750, using that figure would be one solution.

A different approach would be to request from the employer the total hours worked in each of the last three years, and divide annual contributions by annual hours worked, which will provide the desired cents-per-hour figure.

For example:

Year	Annual Contribution	Total Hours Worked	Cents Per Hour Worked
1	$1,200,000	2,000,000	$.60
2	$ 890,000	1,805,000	$.49
3	$ 960,000	1,620,000	$.59

Improvements

The previous section showed how to find the cents-per-hour cost of an existing pension plan. The next skill to learn is how to estimate the per-hour cost of improvements in the pension plan, which is a substantially different matter.

Having followed the previous examples, you realize that when an employer gives a figure for the cost of improving the basic multiplier, this is at best an estimate. The company's per-hour cost is reliable *only if* employment and number of hours worked per employee remain exactly the same; all actuarial assumptions are met exactly with regard to fund earnings, mortality, turnover, and retirement patterns; and none of the actuarial assumptions or cost methods change.

However, the probability of such stability is small. Always keep in mind that cents-per-hour costs in the pension area are very rough estimates and can change considerably in either direction with the stroke of an actuarial pen. It's helpful, though, for a union negotiator to be able to estimate the cost of a basic benefit improvement, if only to help a bargaining committee make decisions about its proposals and priorities. The following simplified procedures might make an actuary smile but are precise enough for what you'll typically use them for.

Estimating the Cost of an Improvement

To estimate the cost of a pension improvement, you'll need the following information:

- Average age of bargaining unit employees
- Average seniority of bargaining unit employees
- Lump sum needed at age 65 to provide $100 a month for life ($100 being used for purposes of example, not because it's an ideal retirement amount)
- Appendix C, Future Values of an Annuity of $1
- Appendix D, The Effect of Age on Pension Cost

As a working example, assume a local of 250 people whose average age is 38 and whose average seniority is 15 years, and that you want to find the cents-per-hour cost of increasing the benefit multiplier from $10 to $11, assuming a work year of 1,800 hours. Use the following procedure:

1. Calculate what the $1 improvement will do to the average individual's basic pension at age 65.

Past service = 15 years × $1 increase = $15 per month at age 65

Future service = 27 years × $1 increase = $27 per month at age 65

Total increase in basic monthly pension = $42 per month at age 65

2. Estimate the lump sum cost of $100 per month for life at age 65 (Appendix D). If you pick a conservative interest rate, such as 6 percent, the lump sum cost of $100 per month is $11,654.40.

3. Use ratios to estimate the cost of the lump sum needed to provide $42 per month. Since $42 per month is 42 percent of the cost of $100 per month, or 42 percent of $11,654, the lump sum

needed at age 65 to pay for the increase in the multiplier is $4,894.68 (.42 × $11,654 = $4,894.68).

4. You know that the cost of the $1 per month benefit improvement will be $4,894.68 for the average member at age 65. How much will have to be put aside each year for the next 27 years (27 years being the amount of time the average member, who is 38, will have to work until retirement)? To calculate this, consult Appendix C, Future Values of an Annuity of $1. Read down the 6 percent column to the 27th row, and you'll find that $1 put aside each year for 27 years at 6 percent will be worth $63.705 at the end of that period. But you need $4,894.68, not $63.70. You'll have to put aside not $1 but $4,894.68 ÷ $63.70 = $76.84 for each member each year. In cents-per-hour terms, that's $76.84 per 2,000 hours ÷ $.038 per hour per $1 increase in the benefit multiplier.

Table 9–2 illustrates the method and shows the cost impact of age and seniority on pension improvements.

Variables that Affect the Calculation

As mentioned earlier, this method of cost estimate has the virtues of simplicity and speed, but there are some shortcomings. The cost estimate frequently is high because this method doesn't account for mortality or turnover. Even with this excess, however, the estimate may come out considerably below that of an actuary.

[*Author's Note*—In one negotiation the union followed this estimating procedure and got a $.04-per-hour cost for each $1 improvement in the benefit multiplier. When the company quoted a cost of $.07, the bargaining committee was distraught. It turned out the company was using a 4.5 percent interest rate assumption and amortizing its past service liability over a dozen years. Because of the short amortization period and low interest rate return, the hourly costs were exceedingly high. This resulted in money going into the fund very fast with a resulting increase in benefit security, but it was like pulling teeth to negotiate a basic benefit improvement at that plant.—J. MacD.]

Further, by using the "average" member for your calculation, you may gloss over some cash flow problems you would encounter in a situation where, for example, half the membership is age 64 with

Table 9–2. Cost Impact of Age and Seniority on Pension Improvements

	Work Force A	Work Force B
Average age	27	45
Average service	3	20
Years to age 65	38	20
Cost of $100 per month at age 65	$11,654	$11,654
Future value of $1 deposited monthly for N years	$135.90	$36.79
	Calculations	
Step 1. $1 per month improvement	$38 future	$20 future
	+3 past	+20 past
	$41	$40
Step 2. Lump sum needed at age 65	41% of $11,654	40% of $11,654
	= $4,778.14	= $4,661.60
Step 3. Annual costs	$4,778.14 ÷ $135.90	$4,661.60 ÷ $36.79
	= $35.16	= $126.71
Step 4. Cents per hour cost	$35.16 ÷ 2000	$126.71 ÷ 2000
	= $.018	= $.063

30 years of service while the other half is a group of 21-year-old new hires.

Calculating for Percent of Earnings Formulas

The preceding approach can be used with percent of earnings formulas, but the arithmetic is more cumbersome because the eventual benefit will be based on a percent of earnings at a point in the future. Therefore, you need to make one extra assumption: what will happen to earnings over time. The following example for an average work force will illustrate:

Average age: 45
Average service: 20 years
Years to age 65: 20

Cost of $100: $11,654
Future value of $1 for 20 years at 6 percent: $36.79

Up to this point the process is identical to the former one. But now additional information is needed in order to calculate the cost:

Current five-year average income, obtained by adding up the past five years' averages and dividing by 5.

Expected final five years' average, calculated by assuming a conservative 4 percent increase each year.

Annual retirement income, obtained through a standard formula: 1 percent × years of service × final five years' average earnings.

As an example, here are the calculations for one local:
Current five-year average income:

$13,000 (five years ago)
13,780 (four years ago)
14,606 (three years ago)
15,483 (two years ago)
16,412 (one year ago)
$73,281

$73,281 ÷ 5 = $14,656 current five-year average

To obtain the expected final five-year average: first multiply $14,656 by 1.04 = $15,242.24. Then multiply $15,242.24 by 1.04, and so on, multiplying the product of each calculation by 1.04 until you reach year 20. The result will be $32,113, which represents the five-year average projected 20 years into the future.

Applying the annual retirement income formula, you can calculate that the annual benefit will be .01 (1 percent) × $32,113 × 40 years (20 past and 20 future, counting from current negotiations) = $12,845.

To obtain the monthly retirement income, divide the annual income by 12 ($12,845 ÷ 12 = $1,070).

To propose an increase in the basic benefit (from 1 percent to 1.1 percent, for example), calculate what the modification will mean in terms of improved monthly benefits if the formula is adopted: .011 (1.1 percent) × $32,113 (average annual income 20 years from now) × 40 years = $14,129.

Monthly retirement income is $14,129 ÷ 12 = $1,177. The difference between the new monthly retirement benefit and old monthly retirement benefit ($1,177 − $1,070) is $107.

To then obtain the lump sum needed at age 65 to pay for benefit improvements, take the ratio of $107 to $100 = $107 ÷ $100 = 1.07 and multiply that by the old standby $11,654: 1.07 × $11,654 = $12,469.78. The process of multiplying $11,654 × 1.07 simply increases $11,654 by 7 percent—the percent the benefit increase of $107 exceeds $100.

To find the annual cost, divide the lump sum by the future value of an annuity of $1 for 20 years: $12,469.78 ÷ $36.79 = $338.94.

From there, divide the annual cost by the hours in the work year for the cost of the improvement: $338.94 ÷ 2000 = $.169 per hour.

As you can see, there are many more unknowns with a percent of earnings formula, all related to the fact that the basic benefit is tied to average earnings at some date in the future.

Early Retirement Benefit Improvements

Consider this hypothetical situation: Your pension plan provides for a normal retirement benefit of $100 a month at age 65, with no provision for retiring earlier than age 65. Individuals who terminate employment before age 65 will have to wait until they reach age 65 to collect their pensions. From Appendix D, as used in calculations earlier in this chapter, you know that the plan will have to have $11,654 set aside for each participant to pay out a benefit of $100 a month beginning at age 65.

The bargaining committee members now want to negotiate a provision for early retirement so that your members can retire when they reach age 64. Is it going to cost more to provide a benefit at age 64 than it would have at age 65?

As you know from the discussion in Chapter 5, the answer is "yes," because people who retire at age 64 will collect their pensions for nearly a year longer, on average, than their counterparts who retire at age 65. In this case, if the benefit is not reduced, they'll be receiving about $1,200 more in benefits in the long run. Further, because their benefit will begin a year earlier, the fund will have a year less to accumulate the needed lump sum, and interest earnings from that year will be forgone.

The combined effect of these factors will vary from plan to plan, but can be as high as an 8 to 9 percent increase in plan costs for each year participants retire before age 65. That is, if it costs the plan

$11,654 to provide $100 a month for life at age 65, it will cost the plan between $12,586 and $12,702 to provide $100 per month for life at age 64 ($11,654 × 1.08 (108 percent) = $12,586.32; $11,654 × 1.09 (109 percent) = $12,702.86).

No-Cost Programs

One way of adjusting for this cost increase in pension plans is through a no-cost program that fixes the age 65 lump sum cost and reduces the benefit level. In the above example, $100 a month benefit would be reduced by 8 percent (assuming the lower of the two cost-increase figures) to $92 a month for life for those who retire at age 64 ($100 × .92 (92 percent) = $92). This $92 benefit will cost the same as $100 per month for life for those who wait until age 65 to retire. Both figures, $92 per month at age 64 and $100 a month at age 65, are called *actuarial equivalents* because they both have the same present, or lump sum, value.

Programs Involving a Cost to the Plan

Other early retirement programs involve a cost to the plan, which must then be funded by increased contributions.

Negotiated modifications of the actuarial adjustments reduce or eliminate the amount of reduction in the accrued normal retirement benefit.

Early retirement supplement programs give the retiree a monthly income supplement to offset the impact of the actuarial reduction. These types of supplements are usually for a short period of time, generally until the employee begins to collect Social Security.

Negotiated Modifications: Estimating the cost for a modification of the actuarial adjustment involves several steps and, as you will see, allows for considerable variation.

To illustrate the procedure, consider the following example:

Benefit at age 65: $100 per month for life
Full actuarial reduction for each year before age 65: 8.5 percent
Current reduced benefit at age 55: $41.13 per month for life
Current hourly cost of the plan: $.60

Union proposal: Replace full actuarial reduction of 8.5 percent with .6 percent for each month prior to age 65 (7.2 percent reduction per year)

Benefit at age 55 under union proposal: $47.36 per month for life

Table 9–3 shows how the current benefit is adjusted for early retirement.

The effects of downward compounding on the union's proposal to change the reduction from 8.5 percent to 7.2 percent would be as indicated in Table 9–4.

To calculate the cost of changing the adjustment from a full actuarial reduction to .6 percent per month prior to age 65 (or 7.2 percent per year), follow this procedure:

1. Calculate the percentage increase in the benefit at the earliest retirement date affected by the change. In the example given previously, the benefit increased from $41.13 at age 55 to $47.36 at age 55, a $6.23, or 15.1 percent, increase.

2. Multiply the current hourly cost of the plan by the percentage increase. In this example, that would be $.60 × .151 (15.1 percent) = $.09 an hour.

Table 9–3. Calculation of Current Actuarially Adjusted Benefit

Age	Dollar Reduction from Preceding Age/Benefit	Monthly Benefit
65	None	$100.00
64	.085 × 100.00 = 8.50	91.50
63	.085 × 91.50 = 7.78	83.72
62	.085 × 83.72 = 7.12	76.60
61	.085 × 76.60 = 6.51	70.09
60	.085 × 70.09 = 5.96	64.13
59	.085 × 64.13 = 5.45	58.68
58	.085 × 58.68 = 4.99	53.69
57	.085 × 53.69 = 4.56	49.13
56	.085 × 49.13 = 4.18	44.95
55	.085 × 44.95 = 3.82	41.13

Table 9-4. Calculation of Benefit Under Union Proposal

Age	Dollar Reduction from Preceding Age/Benefit	Monthly Benefit
65	None	$100.00
64	.072 × 100.00 = 7.20	92.80
63	.072 × 92.80 = 6.69	86.11
62	.072 × 86.11 = 6.20	79.91
61	.072 × 79.91 = 5.75	74.16
60	.072 × 74.16 = 5.34	68.82
59	.072 × 68.82 = 4.96	63.86
58	.072 × 63.86 = 4.59	59.27
57	.072 × 59.27 = 4.27	55.00
56	.072 × 55.00 = 3.96	51.04
55	.072 × 51.04 = 3.67	47.37

3. This figure is the maximum amount that this benefit would cost, because it assumes that everybody retires at age 55 and takes full advantage of the benefit. What's the minimum cost? Zero, should nobody take advantage of the benefit. The actual cost developed by an actuary will vary, depending on the assumptions used concerning early retirement behavior. Actuaries tend to be very conservative in this area; it's not unusual to get cost figures across the bargaining table that are close to the maximum the benefit would cost.

Consider another example, an early retirement provision that has a 6 percent reduction for each year before age 65, with the reduction calculated by multiplying .06 (6 percent) by the years prior to age 65 rather than by the downward compounding method of the previous example. The current cost of the plan is $.36 per hour.

The union proposes to eliminate the reduction for workers who retire at age 62 or after. To calculate the cost:

1. Calculate the benefit increase if everyone took full advantage of the new benefit and retired at age 62. Do this by multiplying 3 years × .06 (6 percent) = .18 (18 percent). By eliminating the 18 percent reduction, you are really increasing the benefit by 18 percent.

2. Multiply the current cost by the percentage increase in the benefit: $.36 × .18 = $.065.

3. The cost of this benefit improvement is between $.00 (if no one uses it) and $.065 per hour (if everyone takes advantage of it).

To refine the above range, you could assume that everyone retired at the average age of retirement assumed in the plan—age 63, for example—and calculate the cost increase for the average person.

1. Calculate the percentage benefit improvement for the average person: .06 × 2 years = .12 (12 percent).

2. Multiply the percent of benefit improvement (12 percent) by the current cost of the plan: .12 × $.36 = $.043. The cost range is between $.00 and $.043 per hour.

As you can see, there can be quite a variation in the cost estimates associated with early retirement benefit improvements.

Early Retirement Supplements: It's difficult to estimate the cost of early retirement supplements because frequently they are not part of the basic pension plan and often are not funded in the usual way. Instead, the company may pay them as a current expense. However, to get a rough approximation of costs, you can use the same approach as that used for the basic benefit.
Consider this example:

Average age: 35
Average seniority: 10 years
Union supplement proposal: $3 a month for each year of credited service to be paid workers who retire before age 62
Supplement ends at age 62 (when Social Security begins)
Early retirement eligibility: age 55 and 10 years service
Years until age 55: 20
Average supplemental benefit available at age 55: $90, or $1,080 per year

Follow this procedure to calculate the cost:

1. Calculate the lump sum needed at age 55 to pay out $1,080 annually for seven years (from age 55 to age 62). Consult Appendix B to find out what is necessary to pay out $1 annually for seven years at the 6 percent interest assumption: $5.582. To find the lump sum needed for $1,080, multiply $1,080 × $5.582 = $6,028.56.

2. Calculate the annual contribution necessary to assure that lump sum 20 years from now, again assuming the 6 percent interest figure. Consult Appendix C: $36.79. Divide this figure into the lump sum needed: $6,028.56 ÷ $36.79 = $163.86, the amount necessary to contribute annually for each participant.

3. Calculate the cents-per-hour contribution. Divide the annual contribution by the average hours worked: $163.86 ÷ 2,000 = $.082 an hour.

4. The cost range of this proposal is from $.00 to $.082 an hour.

As in previous calculations for early retirement reductions, the $.082 represents the maximum cost because it assumes everyone will retire at age 55 with 30 years' service. Nonetheless, it provides an approximate cost to work with.

Both in terms of magnitude and frequency of discussion, the hourly costs of normal retirement benefit improvements and early retirement programs are the major costing problems a negotiator faces in a typical pension negotiation.

Although it isn't possible to discuss every type of plan negotiation that might be at issue during contract talks, some general remarks are in order concerning costs in three additional areas: disability pensions, improved vesting schedules, and employer-paid preretirement surviving spouse coverage.

Disability Pensions

Many pension plans provide some type of total and permanent disability pension. Few people will use this benefit but, to those who need it, it can mean the difference between poverty and a life with limited economic security. Because so few people use the benefit, its cost is far smaller than one might expect for a plan that might have to provide a disabled individual with a monthly income for the bulk of his or her adult life. Table 9–5, which assumes Social Security's definition of total and permanent disability, is based on a major insurance company's estimates, and shows just how small this cost can be.

Note that there is almost no difference between the cost of providing a disability pension with a 10-year eligibility requirement and one with a 15-year eligibility requirement. The different is $.0002 per $1 of monthly benefit. Unfortunately, a number of pen-

Table 9–5. Comparison of Pension and Disability Costs at
Varying Lengths of Service

	Work Force A	Work Force B	Work Force C
Average age	35	40	45
Average service (years)	6.5	9.6	13.4
Cost per hour for benefit of $1 per month per year of credited service at age 65	$.022	$.0318	$.0458
Cost per hour for benefit of $1 per month per year of credited service for participants totally and permanently disabled, with 15 years' service	$.0021	$.0024	$.0032
Same as above, with 10 years' service	$.0023	$.0027	$.0034

sion programs still have a 15-year eligibility requirement. According
to Table 9–5, it costs between one thirtieth and one fiftieth of a cent
to move to a 10-year eligibility requirement.

Further, the cost of adding a disability pension where none
exists is quite small. Unfortunately, there are still union pension
contracts that do not provide for disability coverage through either
the pension plan or long term disability insurance.

Look closely at any company proposals to modify an existing
disability program, such as changes to redefine "total and permanent disability," or changes "to save money." There may be good
reasons to modify administrative rules in a disability program, such
as to eliminate fraudulent claims or to ensure equality of treatment,
but these changes will not have any significant effect on pension
costs.

Vesting

Most negotiated pension plans call for 100 percent vesting after
10 years. To see the cost impact of improving the typical vesting

provision, consider the cost of accelerating full vesting from 10 years to five years in a plan that has a normal retirement benefit of $10 per month per year of service. Because turnover has an impact on vesting costs, the costs in Table 9–6 are given for low, medium, and high turnover rates.

Note that all but one of these figures are below a penny. Clearly, once a contract calls for 100 percent vesting after 10 years, it is not a major cost issue to make improvements. A company may resist a proposed change for other reasons, such as administrative problems or a strong belief that pensions should be reserved for long-term employees. These reasons may be valid from the company's viewpoint, but cost objections are not. Ten-year vesting predominates more because of tradition than for any other reason. When ERISA was adopted, 100 percent vesting at 10 years had become the industry standard; in spite of improvements unions have made at the bargaining table since then, ERISA's minimum standard has somehow become *the* standard. Accelerated vesting schedules should be an important area for plan improvement in the years ahead.

Preretirement Surviving Spouse Provisions

Two major changes in spouse provisions were included in ERISA. The first change made the joint-and-survivor annuity option automatic unless a participant deliberately rejected it at normal retirement. (REACT now makes this automatic unless the *spouse* also rejects it.) The other change required plans to offer a preretire-

---

Table 9–6. Cents per Hour Increase Resulting from Vesting Reduction to Five Years from 10 Years (Based on Benefit of $10 per Month per Year of Service)

Age	Low Turnover	Medium Turnover	High Turnover
35	$.004	$.009	$.013
40	$.002	$.005	$.009
45	$.001	$.003	$.005

ment surviving spouse benefit at early retirement. (REACT expanded this to be effective at time of vesting.)

These changes responded to a specific problem. Before ERISA most negotiated plans required that an individual be at the point of retirement before electing a joint-and-survivor annuity. Individuals who could retire, but who elected not to, had no spouse coverage.

The labor movement fought to make preretirement spouse coverage automatic; unfortunately, the final law went only half way. Every pension plan now has to provide a preretirement surviving spouse option, but plans may actuarially reduce the normal retirement benefit to cover the cost. The typical reduction is around .7 percent for each year it is in effect; therefore a worker who elects the benefit at age 55 and retires at age 65 has his or her normal retirement benefit reduced by 7 percent (.7 percent × 10 years).

As a bargaining committee member, you have the opportunity to eliminate the option and to cover everyone who reaches early retirement eligibility with no reduction in the normal retirement benefit. Under REACT many unions have eliminated the actuarial reduction typically associated with the surviving spouse coverage in effect at the time of vesting.

A quick way to estimate the cost of this benefit is to multiply the current cents-per-hour cost of the plan by the product of years between early retirement eligibility and the normal retirement age times the annual actuarial reduction for surviving spouse coverage (cents per hour × years between early and normal retirement age × reduction for surviving spouse coverage).

Current hourly pension cost: $.60
Early retirement eligibility: Age 55
Normal retirement age: Age 65
Annual actuarial reduction for surviving spouse coverage: .7 percent a year (.007)
Calculations: $.60 × .007 × 10 years = $.042 per hour.

As with all such estimates, this is the maximum cost. Not every 55-year-old has a spouse. Further, the calculation assumes that the benefit will be in effect for all participants for a full 10 years, when some workers won't reach early retirement eligibility until after age 55 because of a time-in-service requirement and others will elect to retire before they reach age 65. Given this limitation, however, this technique can give you an idea of the cost involved.

Pension Costs and Bargaining Strategy

This chapter has given union negotiators some simple tech niques for estimating costs of basic pension plan improvements. The additional pension cost information now available should assist the negotiator in designing better bargaining strategies. How these figures are used in bargaining or in dealing with the membership is a separate matter and will depend on many factors, including the sophistication of the bargaining committee, the economic climate, the company's bargaining style and strategy, and bargaining traditions. Because of these variables, no hard and fast rule governs the use of cost figures in bargaining. However, a few general observations regarding costs are in order.

Focus on Need, not Cost

Keep the bargaining committee focused on needs rather than costs. If it concentrates on costing out proposals, it is likely to start viewing bargaining issues from the point of view of cost accountants rather than union leaders. The committee's first question about a particular proposal then becomes "How much does it cost?" rather than "How well does this meet the members' needs?" A cost focus can misdirect a negotiator from designing strategies that respond to needs.

Try to keep the company away from drawn-out discussions of cost, too. While you have limited control over how a company negotiator handles the other side of the table, there are ways to signal that you're not impressed with the company negotiator's demonstration of simple arithmetic. If the company negotiator insists on long digressions about benefit costs, you can be sure the digressions serve the company's bargaining strategy rather than yours.

Arguing about costs during negotiations is rarely productive. You are unlikely to convince the company to change its method of calculating contract costs. Although at times an argument over costs will have propaganda value for regaining the offensive or defusing a company position, the company's method of accounting for costs is beyond your control.

Because of the variability of pension costs from year to year, be skeptical of any offered trades, such as "$.04 off the last company wage offer for a $1 per-month–per-year-of-service increase in the benefit multiplier." You should evaluate this situation not in terms of whether $.04 will pay for the benefit improvement, but whether the restructuring will produce a better deal for your members. No one knows what $1 per month per year will cost next year or 10 years from now.

Avoid Specific Figures

Union pension negotiators should avoid being too specific on cost figures. Use ranges when discussing costs within the bargaining committee. Once you announce that an improvement will cost $.045, only three things can happen, any of which will cause problems:

- The company's cost will come out lower than your estimate, and you'll immediately be suspected of trying to discourage the committee;
- The company's cost will come out higher than your estimate, leading the committee to suspect the company is lying and diverting the committee to a side issue that is irrelevant to obtaining a contract that's responsive to its members' needs; or
- The company's cost will agree with your estimate, in which case you'll be suspected of conspiring with the company.

Unless it's in the contract that the company is going to contribute at least x cents additional to the pension plan, don't announce at a ratification meeting that the committee agreed to take x cents less in wages and put it into the pension to fund a specific improvement. Invariably someone in the bargaining unit, probably a former committee member or president, will calculate how much is going into the plan; if the plan has had good actuarial experience, the actual contribution might be less than the amount you mentioned. Explaining the intricacies of pension funding to 300 suspicious members is not a comfortable position to find yourself in.

Summary

Remember that collective bargaining is a power process, not an intellectual or rational process. Being able to estimate pension improvement costs gives you only one of the tools you need to make informed negotiating decisions. Unfortunately, the techniques in this chapter cannot make those key decisions for you.

Take, for example, a plant closing in which the bargaining committee and international representative or business agent reach an agreement with the company on terminating the pension plan, with the understanding that excess fund assets will be used to improve benefits. The company's estimate of excess assets and the union's are very close. Given the seniority of the membership and a specific severance formula, it is possible to calculate down to one hundredth of a cent what the severance benefit should be to account for the entire amount.

But what the numbers don't tell the committee is even more important: how much the company might be willing to pay in severance without the redistribution of excess assets. Unfortunately, no calculations exist that can give you the answer to such a question. It is up to you and your skill as a negotiator.

10

Pension Investment Control

In the past four decades, the combined assets of public and private pension plans have grown to $1.4 trillion. With that growth has come increasing scrutiny of groups and institutions that have the authority to direct these funds into various economic activities. Investment control is important both on the level of public policy and the level of individual pension security. The public policy concern centers on who has control, because such control could exercise considerable influence on both the U.S. and world economies. The more personal focus—of more immediate interest to the union negotiator—is whether those in control exercise their authority in a reasonable and intelligent fashion that protects the pension security of current and future retirees.

Although these concerns differ in some respects, in others they are intertwined. Individual retirement security is threatened in a declining economy. Even the current retiree receiving a monthly check from a pension plan sponsored by a healthy, growing company has to worry about Social Security. As the economic pie gets smaller, every economic power group tries to protect its relative share of the nation's wealth. The retiree whose economic security is, in large part, subject to the flux of American politics is in a particularly insecure position.

Ownership Is Not Control

*The Unseen Revolution: How Pension Fund Socialism Came to America,** by Peter Drucker, puts forth the proposition that the

---
*New York: Harper & Row, 1976.

American worker has bought control of the economy by deferring current wages to pension plans, which in turn have purchased a controlling share in the assets of American business.

In a limited sense Drucker is right. Workers have a legally protectable interest in the assets of pension funds; the funds are legally theirs. In turn, these funds own a controlling share of the financial instruments, such as stocks and bonds, outstanding from U.S. corporations. Therefore, workers own American industry. The logic seems solid, but just try cutting down a telephone pole and explaining to the arresting officer that the pole in question is only one of the many that you own because your pension fund owns $1 million in AT&T stock.

Drucker's analysis fails in not distinguishing between ownership and control. It's true that a substantial part of corporate equity and debt has been purchased with the deferred wages of American workers. But it's also true that workers, either individually or through their union representatives, have little effective control over how these deferred wages are invested. Asset management of single-employer pension plans is almost exclusively controlled by employers or their asset managers. The closest that workers come to full control is in the multiemployer Taft-Hartley plans found mainly in the building and construction trades (although isolated examples of joint union-management trusteeship can be found in any heavily organized industry). In these jointly managed funds, investment decisions are made by boards composed of equal numbers of representatives from management and labor.

Even in these plans, however, the degree of direct control over investments varies widely. Most pension plans, including the jointly administered ones, hire professional money managers to make the day-to-day investment decisions. Control depends not on legal relationships spelled out in various contracts, but on how actively union and management trustees investigate, evaluate, and direct the behavior of the professional money managers. An AFL-CIO study, "Investment of Pension Funds,"* reported that in 1979 only $92 billion of an estimated $565 billion in pension fund assets was in jointly controlled plans. The bulk of pension fund money is not subject to control by individual union members or their representatives, and to a large extent is not directly controlled by sponsoring or participating employers, either. Control rests with a relatively small group of financial institutions and managers.

---

*American Federation of Labor and Congress of Industrial Organizations. Washington, D.C.

Why Unions Are Interested in Investment Control

The issue of pension fund investment control is not new; joint control and proposals for a union voice have been around as long as pensions themselves. However, in the past decade the issue has commanded increasingly more attention at all levels of the labor movement, from local unions to the AFL-CIO. The issue has taken on some of the attributes of a cause, with its own proponents, propagandists, experts, and detractors. It has even been a factor in major contract negotiations, most notably the 1979 UAW-Chrysler settlement and the 1984 Machinists' contract with Eastern Airlines.

What has caused this increased attention? There's no simple answer, but several factors have contributed to renewed interest in pension fund control.

First, it's a logical extension of unions' general responsibility to represent the social and economic needs of their members. Careless fund management can cause an erosion of pension plan assets, and while this may not cause any problems in the short term in a healthy industry, it can create payment problems in the event of a plant closing (see Chapter 11). On the other hand, good investment performance, especially in relation to assumed earnings, can lower pension benefit costs and make it easier to negotiate improvements. Therefore, union representatives have a substantial ongoing interest in the investment performance of the pension plans they negotiate. In negotiations, this simple and direct position is difficult for the company negotiator to pick apart. All he or she can say is, "Yes, you're right, but no way are we going to start this."

A second reason for increased interest in joint control has been the growth of defined-contribution pension plans. As noted in Chapter 4, the retirement benefit in a defined-contribution plan depends on the sum of contributions plus earnings. At any contribution level, the benefit depends on investment performance. What is merely a logical extension of union responsibility where a defined-benefit plan is involved becomes almost a minimum standard in a defined-contribution situation. Therefore, to carry out its responsibility to help ensure its members' retirement income security, a union needs to have a voice in the investment decisions.

Third, concession demands by employers, combined with their moves toward union-management cooperation, have sparked the desire for joint control over pension fund assets. While it may be difficult for a management negotiator to argue for joint efforts in one area (quality control, for example) and then turn a deaf ear to union arguments for joint pension investment control, the difficulty, it must be admitted, is only in terms of logic. Unfortunately, consistency doesn't play as large a role in collective bargaining as one might wish. However, in concession bargaining, union proposals on joint control can help gauge the depth of the employer's interest in cooperation.

High unemployment, plant closings, and concerns about Social Security's future also give rise to concern about the security of and desire for control over pension benefits. Although this concern is rarely articulated in chants of "JOINT CONTROL NOW!" at union meetings before the start of negotiations, the concern is nevertheless real.

And finally, as the traditional methods of representing workers and solving work place problems become less effective in the face of antiunion tactics and weak enforcement of federal laws, unions look for new ways to limit the power of corporations. Money being the lifeblood of any company, real control over pension fund assets grows more and more attractive to unions. Several individuals and organizations have explored this topic in recent years, the most notable publication in this area being *The North Will Rise Again: Pensions, Politics, and Power in the 1980's,** by Jeremy Rifkin and Randy Barber, which documents how workers' pension funds are invested in ways contrary to workers' interests.

Preliminary Decisions

Negotiating for joint control over pension fund investment decisions is different from other pension bargaining. You're trying to negotiate a decision-making process, not a specific outcome. It is the distinction, for example, between negotiating a holiday (an outcome) and a grievance and arbitration clause (a process). Remember this, because negotiating a process clause commits the union as an organization to an ongoing, long-term responsibility. Before you negotiate for joint control, give some thought to how this responsibility will be met on a permanent basis.

As in negotiating a grievance and arbitration clause, writing the language into the contract is only the beginning. The language creates a right and a responsibility, but does not guarantee that the process will work. That's up to the local union leadership, who will

---

*Boston: Beacon Press, 1978.

use the process skillfully, ineptly, or not at all. If you are thinking about some type of investment control, a number of areas need careful thought. None of the following questions is earth-shattering, but taken together they indicate that a major organizational commitment is required if the union wants joint control over pension investments.

What efforts will have to be made to train those members who serve on the pension investment committee or board?

Stewards will need training; so will pension representatives. The local should recognize this and support the continuing education of people who serve on the pension committee. The resource commitment is not burdensome, but it is important; joint control will be meaningless unless the union representatives are properly prepared.

The union should commit itself to subscribe to important investment journals and to buy the necessary books for the pension representatives to keep up with developments in the field.

Will the pension representatives be elected or appointed?

There are good arguments for either process; however, serving on a pension committee is different from serving on a bargaining committee. The bargaining committee needs the political backing of the membership to strengthen its negotiating power; therefore, its members should be elected. But injecting local union politics into pension investment decision making could lead to bad results. Local conditions will govern your decision, but remember, the point is to pick a process—whether elective or appointive—that will produce enthusiastic and well-informed representatives.

How long will terms of office be? Should they be staggered to avoid a complete turnover of union representation every few years?

No single answer applies here; however, it will take anybody a certain amount of time and training to function well in the job. Be sure to develop a system that ensures continuity of leadership.

Should an elected union officer, such as the president, also serve as a pension representative?

Again, there is no pat answer; it depends on the activity level of the local union and its degree of organization, its size, and the sophistication of its members.

Preparing to Bargain

In addition to the preparations for bargaining described in Chapter 7, some additional preparations are necessary before negotiating for joint pension control.

Any concern for pension security among the members is unlikely to be focused on the need for joint control. Few of your members have even heard of the issue, let alone formed an opinion on it. Therefore, your first job is to educate them about its importance. You must create a constituency in order to accomplish your purpose at the bargaining table. Management will be sensitive to the membership's level of interest.

Second, you should investigate how current investment decisions are made, and by whom. Does the employer use a bank trust department? An insurance carrier? Some combination of both? How active is the employer in directing the activities of its money managers?

Third, document how well the current system works. What have been the fund earnings over the past several years? Have there been significant losses? How risky is the investment portfolio (how much is in common stock, short- and long-term bonds, and so on)?

Finally, become knowledgeable about the basic fiduciary responsibilities contained in ERISA, and make sure you communicate this knowledge to the bargaining committee. Management may try to scare the bargaining committee into dropping its proposal by having its lawyers give the committee a lengthy discourse on fiduciary responsibility. This is sure to include how full joint control carries with it legal responsibilities that, if not met, can give rise to lawsuits. While the fiduciary responsibilities under ERISA are not particularly burdensome, they can sound scary to a bargaining committee if it is first made aware of them while sitting at the bargaining table.

Anyone who exercises discretionary control over the operation of a pension plan and its assets is a *fiduciary*. There are two basic criteria—or fiduciary standards—that apply to investing pension assets: decisions have to be prudent or reasonable, and they have to be in the interests of the plan participants. Another way of phrasing the latter standard is that investment decisions can't be fraudulent or self-interested—you can't, for example, give your brother an interest-free loan from the fund. As an example of the prudence standard, assets should be invested to avoid sudden sharp losses in value—don't put all your assets in real estate development in a concentrated area of a single city.

There's a lot written about fiduciary responsibility and standards; remember that anyone of average intelligence, judgment, and honesty can meet the requirements with little difficulty.

Bargaining Strategy

In addition to the strategies discussed in previous chapters, a few observations pertinent to bargaining for joint control are in order.

Before discussing the specifics of any arrangement with the management bargaining team, try to get an agreement in principle that the union should have a voice in investment decisions. It doesn't make sense to argue about details until management indicates that it is willing to work toward joint control. Don't let the company negotiator draw you into a "what if" conversation. You're negotiating a process, not the results of that process.

Avoid discussing "social investing." Although the phrase describes a legitimate and important concept, it is likely to be a red flag at the bargaining table. The general concept implies investment policies that, in addition to return and risk, take into account social considerations, such as whether a specific investment will promote employment in a given industry, or the labor relations or occupational health records of corporations. The investment board or committee may want to consider investment decisions that might be termed "social investing," but these decisions should be made by those who have overall responsibility for the fund assets, not by union and company negotiators.

What to Negotiate

In order to negotiate for joint control over investments, you need to have a clear idea what such contract language looks like. Appendix M provides a sample of joint control language. Don't consider this as the model language, because it's only one of many possible arrangements. For a good collection of different approaches, subscribe to *Labor and Investments* (see "Pension Language," in Chapter 7).

You may want to consider different approaches to and levels of union involvement with pension fund asset control. Several approaches are described below.

Contract language that requires the company to provide the union with detailed financial reports regarding the operation of the pension fund:

This approach carries with it the least amount of control because all that is established is the right to be informed. However, this can be an important first step toward gaining joint control. It provides the information needed to educate the bargaining committee and the members about the operation of the fund. Further, the union's active monitoring of investment decisions may cause the employer to make those decisions more carefully.

Information recommended by the AFL-CIO's Industrial Union Department for evaluating investment performance includes:

- A list of the investments of the fund
- The earnings of each investment
- The original purchase price and current market value of each investment
- The identity of firms managing the fund and fees paid to such managers
- The relationships between firms managing the fund and financial institutions servicing the employer
- An itemized breakdown of the cost of administering the fund
- Any instructions that the trustees have given to money managers
- A record of how stock voting rights have been exercised*

Contract language that requires financial reports and an annual meeting of the pension committee and the fund administrator, actuary, and money manager:

This is also only a "right-to-know" clause, but it brings the union one step closer to direct involvement in investment decisions. Having a forum in which you can ask questions and explore the thinking that went into plan investments marks a major step from merely receiving reports about plan operations. And, of course, at the forum there's nothing to prevent you from making recommendations; they may be nonbinding but there's a chance they'll influence subsequent investment decisions.

---

*Source: Industrial Union Dep't, AFL-CIO Report on Benefit Investment Policies. May, 1980.

If you follow this approach, make sure the contract language contains a requirement that all relevant reports be provided well in advance of the meeting, to allow you to evaluate them and prepare your questions.

The next logical step is to establish an arrangement such as that in Appendix M, which creates a committee whose duties are mostly advisory, but which has a good deal of clout. The responsibilities for carrying out the terms of the pension plan are divided among four entities in this example:

- The board, in this case the company
- The administrative committee, consisting of one representative each from union and management
- The administrator
- The trustee

Each entity has certain specific responsibilities. The board has the responsibility of hiring the administrator, who will handle the day-to-day operation of the plan. The trustee has the responsibility for the daily management of the fund assets. The administrative committee has the responsibility "for appointing and removing any investment managers, for monitoring the performance of any investment managers, for determining a funding policy and investment objectives for the Plan, and for determining any benefit claims appeals."

This language gives the union a measure of control over the investment of its pension fund money while limiting the union representative's responsibility for daily operations.

There are many possible variations. For example, the administrative committee could appoint the administrator, the trustee, or both. Or, the administrative committee could be the named trustee with the responsibilities of all four entities.

[*Author's Note*—You'll note that in the sample language the administrative committee has the authority to develop investment guidelines, but is precluded from making investments or directing specific investments. Although a degree of control is lost, this limit has some advantages. At the location where the above language was negotiated, when it became public knowledge that the union had obtained a voice in investment decisions, one bank in town actually sent someone into the plant to talk with the union members. The bank official was discovered walking around inside the plant, glad-handing like a politician as he asked workers to "vote"for his bank. His campaign didn't last long; he was soon hustled from the plant.

That's an extreme case, but it illustrates the need to build checks and balances into the investment control process. At the above location, the administrative committee (and thus the union) did not have the authority to make specific investments; therefore, it was immune to the type of pressure the banker was trying to generate.—J. MacD.]

Pension fund asset investment and control is one of the more exciting areas of pension bargaining. This brief treatment provides a glimpse for union representatives who are willing to take the time and effort to become well-informed in this area.

11

Pension Negotiations During a Plant Closing

With any kind of luck, you'll never have to go through a plant closing. A plant closing is traumatic not only for the workers and the community, but for the bargaining committee, which must try to negotiate pension protection. Pensions are designed to exist in perpetuity; trying to close down an agreement, knowing there is no "next round" of negotiations to gain needed improvements, leaves you with a terrible sense of finality. You're no longer bargaining for the abstract "retiree"; you're trying to salvage something for Joe, who's been at the plant for 28 years, and for Marylou, who is the sole support of her four children. The results of a termination are likely to be both unpredictable and harmful to the plan participants, and often there's little the committee can do to help; after all, your bargaining power isn't what it used to be.

When to Negotiate Pension Rights

Federal law requires an employer to bargain over the effects of a plant closing, which means that an employer has to sit down and discuss issues such as severance pay, relocation rights, and pension benefits with the union. However, the law does not require a *settlement*, only bargaining. When a plant is closing, a union's bargaining power falls dramatically because it is hardly likely to strike. The union is not powerless, however; the efficient and economical closing of a facility requires the cooperation of the union and its members. Expensive equipment has to be protected, dismantled, and moved; ongoing commitments to customers must be honored. It's not unusual, in fact, for a company to recall workers from layoff shortly after a plant closing has been announced.

Still, the best time to negotiate good pension protections in a plant shutdown is when the facility is healthy. That's when you have the power to negotiate good language.

The absolute worst time to negotiate is when a facility is tottering on the brink of closing, before a decision has been made. The employer is likely to respond to your model proposal with only a minimum "starter" program, such as a token severance, a one-month extension of health insurance, and no improvements in pension benefits or relocation rights. You're right to suspect there may not be any future negotiations to build on that start. However, it's very difficult to turn down a starter program in the hope of being able to negotiate something better when and if the plant closes. On the other hand, if, as is likely, you reach an agreement, the company will be able to argue that it has complied with its obligation to bargain over "effects" if the plant does close.

Therefore, the best time to negotiate good plant-closing language is before the employer has reason to be concerned. Unfortunately, when a plant is healthy, plant-closing language is unlikely to be high on the members' list of priorities. As with pension investment control, making this an issue depends on the committee's leadership and education of the membership.

Information the Union Needs to Obtain

Once a plant closing has been announced, the necessity of bargaining for each individual member gives the whole negotiation a highly personal character. You'll notice this especially regarding early retirement eligibility, which may have implications for health insurance coverage and basic pension benefits. A worker's vesting status may determine whether he or she will ever receive any further benefits. Dates for disability eligibility are likewise critical. When you begin bargaining, all these dates can be negotiated. Recognizing that there always will be someone left out, make it your goal to get as many people as many benefits as possible. Even if you only manage to protect one additional person, it's worth the effort.

The first place to start when you're preparing to negotiate a plant-closing agreement is with a breakdown of the bargaining unit members by age, vesting service, benefit service, seniority, and hours credited to date in current plan years. Examine the impact of any existing or proposed eligibility rule. Are there any members who could be helped by small modifications in the eligibility rules? Are there one or two people who could be helped by adjusting the dates?

For example, eligibility may be tied to being an active employee on the date the plant closing was announced. You discover that one member had gone on involuntary layoff just three days earlier because of a long-term degenerative illness. You should negotiate for the date to be moved back four days.

Another example would be where the company proposes that for early retirement with full health care coverage, eligibility be based on attainment of 10 years' service and age 55 by September 1 of the current year (which terminates the current agreement three months after the plant closes). Again, by looking at the breakdown, you find three employees with extended service who won't become age 55 until September 5, 11, and 22, respectively. You should try to get the company to extend the deadline until September 30.

You can't begin to make specific proposals of this sort until you know where your members stand. Although some member is always going to complain that eligibility should have been extended one more day or one more month or one more year, just remember that you did what you could in a bad situation. Accepting the eligibility rules as proposed by management would have been a greater evil, and your other option would have been not to try at all.

Responding to the Company's Announcement

Because pensions are designed as long-term programs and are funded on a long-term basis, at any given time there may be some unfunded liability. This is especially likely in negotiated plans that call for regular benefit improvements in both future and past service. When a plant closes, there's always a probability that this long-term program will be terminated,* possibly at a time short of full

---

*The process of terminating a pension plan is an involved and sometimes lengthy process which is begun when an employer notifies the PBGC of its intent to terminate a plan at some future date (no earlier than 10 days after the notice is filed). The practical effect of a termination is that the plan ceases to exist as a legal entity. The assets of the fund are distributed to the participants—almost always in the form of individual annuities—according to guidelines which are contained in the text of ERISA, Title IV, Subtitle C, Section 4044. Distribution is usually accomplished by using plan assets to purchase annuities from commercial insurance companies.

Prior to the termination, it was the pension plan which had the legal obligation for the accumulated pension promises. After the termination, it is usually the issuer of the annuity contract who has the legal obligation to provide the promised pension benefits. Sometimes an employer will decide not to terminate a plan during a plant closure. This is fairly rare because of administration costs and the continued obligation to pay PBGC premiums. In this rare case, the plan and fund continue in operation as though the plant closure had not occurred. The promises and the obligation to fulfill them remain with the ongoing plan.

funding. On the date the plant closing is announced officers will start receiving phone calls from members who ask: "What's going to happen to my pension benefit?" and "Will I get my full benefit?"

The union leadership's best answer at this point is that it does not know but will make every effort to guarantee full benefits. The result will depend on the complex relationships between the frequency and size of recent pension benefit increases, the minimum guarantees of the Pension Benefit Guaranty Corporation (PBGC), the wording of the current labor agreement, the level of assets in the fund, the present value of the plan liability at the actuarial rate of interest and at the termination rate used by the commercial insurance carriers, and most importantly, the company's posture at the bargaining table, which will depend on all of these factors.

The easiest way to understand the workings of these relationships is to take a sample situation and walk through the possibilities.

On September 1, the company calls in the local union officers and tells them the parent company is going to close this particular plant six months from today. The bargaining committee immediately schedules a meeting in two weeks to discuss with the company the effects of the plant closing. On the 2nd, the committee asks the company for the information it needs, which arrives by the end of the week. On the 14th, the committee and the company meet.

For the sake of simplicity, consider for the time being only what you have to do to maintain and protect the members' accumulated pension benefits. First, review the pension contract. If you haven't negotiated plant-closing language in previous contracts, you're likely to find language to the effect that the employer's liability toward the contractually agreed-on benefits is limited to the assets in the fund at the time of termination. This means that the employer is not responsible for providing full benefits.

Your next step is to draft a proposal that eliminates this limitation of the employer's liability. This can be accomplished with this sentence:

> "The employer agrees to guarantee accrued pension benefits at 100 percent for all participants, including both vested and nonvested employees."

This proposal says that the employer will add whatever extra contributions are necessary to ensure that everyone gets his or her accumulated pension.

How the Company Can React

Table 11–1 illustrates the employer's three possible responses. In the first two instances, the effects are clear. In the first scenario,

Table 11-1. Possible Company Responses to Union Proposal for Guarantee of 100% of Accrued Benefits

Union proposal: All accumulated benefits to be guaranteed to be paid in full by the employer

Company response:	*Agreement*	*Partial agreement*	*Refusal*
Results:	Both vested and nonvested participants receive 100% of accumulated benefits.	Will keep plan in effect but with no change in vesting; full benefits for vested employees, no benefits for non-vested employees	Will terminate plan effective Day X Either: Assets will be insufficient to cover Pension Benefit Guaranty Corporation's minimum guarantees, so nonvested employees will lose all benefits; vested employees may have pension reduced. Or: Assets will be sufficient that vested employees will get 100% of benefits but nonvested employees will lose all benefits. Or: Assets will be sufficient to pay both vested employees and nonvested employees full benefits.

the company agrees to guarantee all benefits. You may tell all your members that they will receive all their benefits. In the second scenario, the company agrees to maintain the pension as it is (that is, not terminate it). Employees who are vested will receive 100 percent of their benefits; those who are not vested before termination of service will lose their accumulated benefits. Your strategy according to this scenario might be either to improve the vesting rule to cover more people, or to try to negotiate additional pension service so that more people can meet the current, unmodified rule.

The last set of possibilities, when the company decides to terminate the plan and you are unable to modify this position through negotiation, leads to the most ambiguous results. How the benefits are distributed will depend largely on the level of assets and the relationship between benefits specified in the contract and PBGC guaranteed minimums. It may be that everyone, vested and nonvested, will receive full benefits because of the level of assets. However, as indicated in the first possibility under this scenario, even vested participants may receive a benefit reduction because of insufficient assets and a benefit which is in excess of the PBGC guarantees.

Limits on the Company's Right to Terminate

Can the company really terminate the plan? In many cases, it can—many single-employer pension plans give the employer the clear right to do so. However, frequently the labor agreement has language that restricts the right to terminate prior to the agreement's expiration. In these cases you may argue that it's a violation of the labor agreement to terminate the plan.

Unfortunately, ERISA did not address the issue of whether an existing labor agreement bars a pension plan termination. Under current law, the existence of a labor agreement will not prevent the PBGC from processing and terminating a pension plan. Therefore, once the employer has notified the PBGC of its intent to terminate the plan (as federal law requires), the union's recourse is either to arbitrate or to file an unfair labor practice charge. In both cases the question becomes whether there are any implied or actual contractual limits placed on the company's right to terminate the plan. There are four language situations you as a negotiator might encounter that have a bearing on this:

1. The qualified pension plan gives the company the right to terminate the pension plan, and there is no reference to the pension

in the basic labor agreement. The company decides to close the plant one year into a three-year agreement.

2. The situation is the same as above, except that the pension agreement is outlined in the three-year contract.

3. The qualified pension plan gives the company the right to terminate "subject to the terms of the three-year labor contract." The labor contract is silent regarding the pension plan.

4. The situation is the same as in No. 3, except that the labor contract specifically states that the company is prohibited from terminating the pension plan before the termination of the labor contract.

It's arguable that in all four situations the company cannot terminate the pension plan until the contract expires. However, the question isn't whether the case is arguable; the question is whether it's arguable and viable before either an arbitrator or a judge. The only situation relatively free from ambiguity on this point is the fourth one—the other three are cloudy, the worst being the first and the most common being the second.

The ideal situation, of course, is No. 4, where there's a specific prohibition against terminating the plan. However, there are some very practical problems in getting that kind of language at the bargaining table, and enforcing it if you get it. In the first place, most bargaining committees don't discover the termination clause in the pension plan until they're worried about a plant shutdown. At this point the company has finally admitted publicly that the plant might be going under and has strengthened its resolve not to undertake long-term financial commitments such as funding a pension plan for three more years. Further, the union is in no position to strike over a "what if" issue such as the company's right to terminate the plan. The irony is that when the committee thinks it needs this kind of language, it will be unlikely to get it through collective bargaining or any other process. This language should have been negotiated when times were good.

On an even more practical level, even where you have limitations on termination rights, when a plant is about to close the employer usually conditions other benefits (as, for example, severance pay and health insurance) on the union's agreement to eliminate the limitation. Because of this, limitations aren't particularly valuable in preventing plan terminations; instead, they provide you with power over something the company wants and needs: the right to terminate the pension plan. This increases your limited bargaining power.

The Role of the PBGC

When the company has the clear right to terminate, and does, what happens next depends on the PBGC. The PBGC, which was established with the passage of ERISA, insures accumulated pension benefits against loss. But it does not insure against all loss, only against a minimum amount. Further, the PBGC only guarantees payments to vested participants; it provides no protection for nonvested benefits. The PBGC operates similarly to an insurance company in that it collects premiums from pension plans. When a company terminates a plan without having sufficient assets to meet its minimum guarantees, the PBGC takes responsibility for the minimum payment.

The point to remember about the PBGC is that it provides a minimum guarantee, not a 100 percent guarantee of accumulated pension benefit. The guarantee is phased in at a rate of 20 percent or $20 per month (whichever is greater) per year that a benefit is in effect. Therefore, after a benefit rate is in effect for five years, it is 100 percent guaranteed.

The difficulty of determining at what level benefits are guaranteed can be seen if you take a local which has improved benefits by between $.50 and $1 in each of the last five years, according to this schedule: $.50 the first year, then $1, $.75, $1, and $1. Each of these separate increases would be at a different level of the phase-in, and the guarantees would differ depending on each individuals' years of service.

Some plans will have more than adequate assets to meet all the vested and nonvested liability. In those cases not only will vested participants be paid their benefits, but nonvested participants will receive their benefits as well.

All this is only to say that if the employer insists on terminating a negotiated pension plan there is little you can tell a participant except that minimum guarantees for vested benefits exist and, if there are sufficient assets, all or a portion of nonvested benefits will be provided.

Proposals to Make During a Plant Closing

You should prepare to negotiate regarding pensions in a plant closing much as you would for any negotiation, adding to your letter requesting information the additional request for "hours accumulated to date of announcement of closing." However, any proposals will differ from the normal negotiation in that they will deal directly with retirement problems created by the closing.

The most basic proposal is the *guarantee of payment of 100 percent of accrued benefits for both vested and nonvested participants*, which insures that, at the time a facility closes, all participants are guaranteed their accrued benefit regardless of their years of service or the status of the fund. Although the PBGC guarantees certain minimum benefits, these guarantees are phased in over time and it's not infrequent for members to have a PBGC benefit smaller than 100 percent of their accrued benefit. Further, the PBGC guarantees only vested benefits; it does not make payments to unvested participants. In a plan termination everybody is 100 percent vested for the purpose of distributing plan assets; frequently, however, there are no assets to distribute to nonvested participants, who lose their accrued but nonvested benefit.

The second proposal to negotiate is *elimination of any actuarial reduction for early retirement*. In a work place that remains open, the decision to retire early is voluntary except in the case of poor health. The presumption is that those who exercise the right to retire early have looked at their finances and have decided that they are financially secure even with the reduction in the basic benefit. However, when a plant closes, older workers frequently exercise their early retirement rights simply to put food on the table; there may be no jobs for someone over 50. In this situation the pension program becomes an extended unemployment compensation program. If actuarial reductions are not eliminated, a worker forced into early retirement at a young age (55 or so) will suffer a substantial permanent reduction in the basic benefit.

Another proposal aimed at the older worker calls for *special early retirement eligibility rules for people with extended service and/or older age*. These provisions are designed because older workers usually have a more difficult time finding a new job after a plant shutdown. Such a proposal could include early retirement eligibility at age 50 and 10 years of service, or eligibility if the sum of a worker's age and service is equal to or greater than age 65 (for example, age 45 and 20 years of service). Again, these provisions are far more meaningful if reduction factors are eliminated.

It's helpful, too, to *eliminate the "active" employee requirement for preretirement surviving spouse benefits*. While these are usually reserved for employees who actually are working, many individuals may not wish to exercise their right to retire early but would like this benefit. An attempt should be made to get this type of coverage.

A proposal providing for *vesting and benefit service accrual after permanent layoff* creates what is sometimes called "drift," because its major purpose is to help people "drift" into benefit eligibility after the plant is closed. Obviously, the company would like to cut off service accrual with the date of permanent layoff. The easiest bargaining situation regarding service accrual occurs when a plan has an elapsed time method of measuring service. The plan should already call for vesting and benefit accrual for 12 months of layoff, so it might not require modification. Where the hours-counting method is used, you may have to negotiate a specific modification to grant credit for hours lost in any given year due to a plant shutdown.

If the company refuses to guarantee all benefits, there are two advantages to a proposal to *limit the employer's right to terminate the plan for the duration of the agreement.* First, if the plant closes during the term of the agreement, the company will have an obligation to continue to fund the past service liability—the more money in the fund, the more secure the benefits. Second, the PBGC's guaranteed payments increase according to a sliding scale based on the time from the date of benefit adoption until the termination date. Extending the termination date may raise the PBGC guarantees to a higher percentage rate or even 100 percent of vested benefits.

It makes sense to propose that after all plan liabilities are satisfied, *excess assets should revert to the participants in the form of improved benefits.* If you allow excess assets to be used for any other purpose, such as severance, you can never tell whether you have just provided the company with money it may have been willing to provide anyway.

In plant closings where the plan is anywhere close to being fully funded under the current actuarial assumption, *get competitive bids from commercial insurance carriers on purchasing the assets and liabilities.* If a fund has a serious asset deficiency you're unlikely to be able to improve benefits, but with a healthy fund there is a possibility of improving benefits through competitive bidding because the interest rates used by the carriers to figure liabilities may be significantly higher than the plan interest rate assumption. For example, suppose that before a plan termination the present value of all accrued liability in a fund was $7 million using a 7 percent discount, and the assets in the fund are $7 million. The discount rate is the rate of return you assumed on existing assets; that is, if the $7 million earns 7 percent a year, there will be just enough to pay off the liabilities. If the existing assets earned more than 7 percent, you would need less than $7 million to buy off all the liabilities. A commercial insurance carrier could provide the promised benefits at a price far lower than $7 million if it bid using a 9 or 10 percent discount. Insurance carriers can use the higher rate because the benefits allow them to match investment to the needed cash flow. At least in the current market this allows for considerably lower liability estimates, thus freeing assets for improved benefits.

12

Bargaining Agenda for the Future

Because of the diversity of the private pension system, it's difficult to develop one set of bargaining goals that will fit every plan. What works for one defined-benefit plan might not work for another, and what fits most defined-benefit plans may be completely inappropriate for a defined-contribution plan.

Further, the benefits and language already in your plan affect what you can do in the next round of negotiations. If anything can be said with certainty regarding the collective bargaining process, it is that change occurs slowly rather than in leaps and bounds.

With these cautions in mind, study the pension issues and goals in this chapter that apply to the plan or plans with which you're involved. You'll have to evaluate each suggestion on its own merits in relation to your plan, differentiating between what is important in the ideal world and what is attainable in your situation.

Agenda for Defined-Benefit Plans

The following is a list of general goals that should apply in negotiating a defined-benefit plan.

Participation should be immediate upon hire or at the end of the probationary period. Immediate participation is common in negotiated contracts, but there still are too many that contain age or service requirements. Participation should be counted toward both vesting and benefit accrual.

Vesting should be 100 percent after five years of service. As mentioned in Chapter 9, the cost of this change is relatively small and, while it will not affect long-service employees, it's a step in the right direction in providing adequate benefits for workers who change employers with some regularity. It is time for pension programs to recognize that American workers frequently change jobs.

Vesting service should continue to accrue for the length of seniority during a layoff, and *benefits should continue to accrue* for one year from the date of layoff. If your plan uses an hours-counting system, a participant should be credited with hours while on layoff until severance of seniority for vesting purposes occurs, and for one year for benefit accrual purposes. Participants should be credited with hours towards vesting and benefit accrual while on approved medical leaves of absence. In other words, pension language should assure that all employees with a permanent, continuing employment relationship will receive full crediting of service.

The union should be provided yearly with *all reports necessary for informed bargaining,* including the actuarial report, the trustees' report, the DOL 5500, and a report on vesting and benefit service accumulation, by participant, for the previous year. This information is available to the union negotiator by law without specific language, but it's preferable to have it as an automatic contractual right.

Pension claims administration should be handled by a joint union-management committee. This allows the union to place its support behind the individual participant when he or she applies for a pension. Further, it builds a better information base in the local union, which will help in preparing to negotiate.

Dispute resolution should be handled through binding arbitration. Many pension agreements still do not include dispute resolution procedures that call for the use of a neutral third party with the authority to issue binding decisions.

Early retirement eligibility should begin at age 55 with 10 years of service. The benefit should be unreduced beginning at age 62, the Social Security eligibility date. This is one of those benefit areas where the goals are unlimited; there's nothing magic about age 55 and 10 years, or unreduced benefits at age 62. However, the actual early retirement age eligibility requirement doesn't have much significance for most workers because they can't afford to retire before they're eligible for Social Security. For the same reason, most of the bargaining attention on early retirement actuarial reductions should be focused on the years between age 62 and 65.

The Retirement Equity Act of 1984 made it mandatory that qualified pension plans offer an automatic preretirement surviving spouse benefit to all vested participants. It left open the question of who pays for the benefit: the plan or the participant. Your goal should be to provide *coverage with no reduction in the normal or early retirement benefit* (that is, the company should pay for the coverage through increased contributions). Short of achieving this, try to provide coverage at no cost to the employee upon reaching early retirement eligibility.

Eliminate age requirements and reduce service requirements to vesting requirements for disability provisions, because members frequently become disabled after only short periods of service. Further, a minimum pension based on a percentage of income is a valuable pension improvement. The plan should provide that if an individual on a total and permanent disability pension should be deemed ineligible, his or her seniority should be fully reinstated so that the member can exercise recall rights.

Eliminate career average and future-service-only methods for calculating normal retirement benefits. These methods are popular with employers because they cost less, but cheap plans mean low benefits. What is an adequate benefit level? It's not unreasonable to assert that workers should have retirement income, including Social Security, that provides for a standard of living roughly equivalent to that attained in their last year of work.

Benefit and service accrual for workers who continue to work after normal retirement age should either be full, actuarially increased yearly, or, at a minimum, based on the multiplier in effect at the actual retirement date. Designing a goal in this area is difficult because of different philosophies about encouraging work past age 65; however, the underlying principle is that someone should not be made worse off as a result of deciding to work beyond the normal retirement age. Freezing the accumulated benefit at the normal retirement eligibility date has this effect.

Prohibit funding waiver applications to the IRS during the term of the contract. This is not to say that a company won't find itself in a financial bind that would justify a funding waiver; the prohibition merely dictates that the company will include the union in the decision-making process.

Prohibit plan terminations for the term of the contract. This goal is similar to the previous one in that it gives the union additional bargaining power. Also negotiate for a provision stating that if there are excess assets in the fund at termination (after all liabilities have been satisfied), assets should revert to the participants in the form of improved pension benefits.

In the event of a partial or complete plant closing, you should try to achieve the following for your members:

- Employer's guarantee to pay 100% percent of all accrued benefits, both vested and nonvested
- Elimination of any actuarial reduction at early retirement
- Reduction of the early retirement eligibility to age 50
- Elimination of the employee status requirement for the pre-retirement surviving spouse benefit

Pension investment control. The union should seek full joint control over investments, either through joint trusteeship or pension investment committees with authority to hire and fire investment managers, to ensure that assets are invested conservatively.

Agenda for Defined-Contribution Plans

Negotiating for defined-contribution plans calls for a different set of goals.

Participation should be immediate upon hire or at the end of the probationary period.

Vesting should be immediate or after three years. Federal law allows a defined-contribution plan to defray administrative costs with money from forfeitures. For this reason, some plans have limited vesting rules, such as three or five years for 100 percent vesting.

Target employer hourly contributions so that the individual's principal plus interest will be approximately the same at the normal retirement age regardless of a worker's current age. The employer accordingly will contribute more for older workers than for younger ones, whose accounts will earn interest to make up the difference.

Hours crediting should be based on hours compensated plus time on layoff for up to one year, plus nonpaid medical leaves of absence. In a defined-contribution plan it is important to review carefully the hours for which contributions will be made. This recommendation is designed to give those employees who have a permanent relationship with the employer a full year's contribution for each year that a relationship exists.

The union should negotiate a *supplemental long-term disability program* that provides a percentage of income replacement for life for workers who are totally and permanently disabled.

Limit cash-out of individual accounts to those who sever seniority rights. Pension plans should provide for retirement, not income supplements for active workers. Negotiating this recommendation limits the right to liquidate a pension to workers who will not be returning to active service in the bargaining unit.

Appendix A. Components of a Defined-Benefit Pension Plan

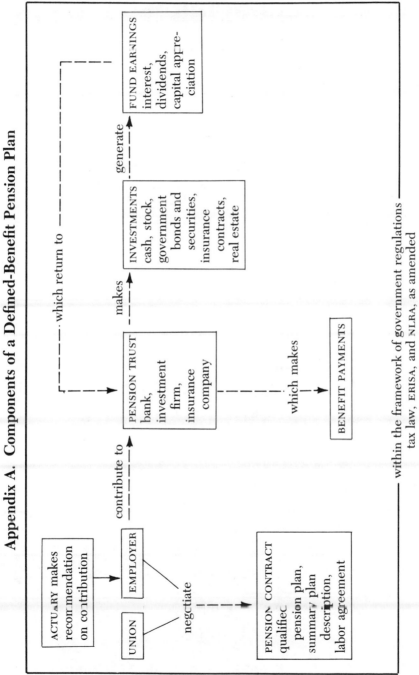

Appendix B. Present Value of $1 Received Annually for N Years

Years (N)	1%	2%	4%	6%	8%	10%	12%	14%	15%	16%	18%	20%	22%	24%	25%	26%	28%	30%	35%	40%	45%	50%
1	0.990	0.980	0.962	0.943	0.926	0.909	0.893	0.877	0.870	0.862	0.847	0.833	0.820	0.806	0.800	0.794	0.781	0.769	0.741	0.714	0.690	0.667
2	1.970	1.942	1.886	1.833	1.783	1.736	1.690	1.647	1.626	1.605	1.566	1.528	1.492	1.457	1.440	1.424	1.392	1.361	1.289	1.224	1.165	1.111
3	2.941	2.884	2.775	2.673	2.577	2.487	2.402	2.322	2.283	2.246	2.174	2.106	2.042	1.981	1.952	1.923	1.868	1.816	1.696	1.589	1.493	1.407
4	3.902	3.808	3.630	3.465	3.312	3.170	3.037	2.914	2.855	2.798	2.690	2.589	2.494	2.404	2.362	2.320	2.241	2.166	1.997	1.849	1.720	1.605
5	4.853	4.713	4.452	4.212	3.993	3.791	3.605	3.433	3.352	3.274	3.127	2.991	2.864	2.745	2.689	2.635	2.532	2.436	2.220	2.035	1.876	1.737
6	5.795	5.601	5.242	4.917	4.623	4.355	4.111	3.889	3.784	3.685	3.498	3.326	3.167	3.020	2.951	2.885	2.759	2.643	2.385	2.168	1.983	1.824
7	6.728	6.472	6.002	5.582	5.206	4.868	4.564	4.288	4.160	4.039	3.812	3.605	3.416	3.242	3.161	3.083	2.937	2.802	2.508	2.263	2.057	1.883
8	7.652	7.325	6.733	6.210	5.747	5.335	4.968	4.639	4.487	4.344	4.078	3.837	3.619	3.421	3.329	3.241	3.076	2.925	2.598	2.331	2.108	1.922
9	8.566	8.162	7.435	6.802	6.247	5.759	5.328	4.946	4.772	4.607	4.303	4.031	3.786	3.566	3.463	3.366	3.184	3.019	2.665	2.379	2.144	1.948
10	9.471	8.983	8.111	7.360	6.710	6.145	5.650	5.216	5.019	4.833	4.494	4.192	3.923	3.682	3.571	3.465	3.269	3.092	2.715	2.414	2.168	1.965
11	10.368	9.787	8.760	7.887	7.139	6.495	5.937	5.453	5.234	5.029	4.656	4.327	4.035	3.776	3.656	3.544	3.335	3.147	2.752	2.438	2.185	1.977
12	11.255	10.575	9.385	8.384	7.536	6.814	6.194	5.660	5.421	5.197	4.793	4.439	4.127	3.851	3.725	3.606	3.387	3.190	2.779	2.456	2.196	1.985
13	12.134	11.343	9.986	8.853	7.904	7.103	6.424	5.842	5.583	5.342	4.910	4.533	4.203	3.912	3.780	3.656	3.427	3.223	2.799	2.468	2.204	1.990
14	13.004	12.106	10.563	9.295	8.244	7.367	6.628	6.002	5.724	5.468	5.008	4.611	4.265	3.962	3.824	3.695	3.459	3.249	2.814	2.477	2.210	1.993
15	13.865	12.849	11.118	9.712	8.559	7.606	6.811	6.142	5.847	5.575	5.092	4.675	4.315	4.001	3.859	3.726	3.483	3.268	2.825	2.484	2.214	1.995
16	14.718	13.578	11.652	10.106	8.851	7.824	6.974	6.265	5.954	5.669	5.162	4.730	4.357	4.033	3.887	3.751	3.503	3.283	2.834	2.489	2.216	1.997
17	15.562	14.292	12.166	10.477	9.122	8.022	7.120	6.373	6.047	5.749	5.222	4.775	4.391	4.059	3.910	3.771	3.518	3.295	2.840	2.492	2.218	1.998
18	16.398	14.992	12.659	10.828	9.372	8.201	7.250	6.467	6.128	5.818	5.273	4.812	4.419	4.080	3.928	3.786	3.529	3.304	2.844	2.494	2.219	1.999
19	17.226	15.678	13.134	11.158	9.604	8.365	7.366	6.550	6.198	5.877	5.316	4.844	4.442	4.097	3.942	3.799	3.539	3.311	2.848	2.496	2.220	1.999
20	18.046	16.351	13.590	11.470	9.818	8.514	7.469	6.623	6.259	5.929	5.353	4.870	4.460	4.110	3.954	3.808	3.546	3.316	2.850	2.497	2.221	1.999
21	18.857	17.011	14.029	11.764	10.017	8.649	7.562	6.687	6.312	5.973	5.384	4.891	4.476	4.121	3.963	3.816	3.551	3.320	2.852	2.498	2.221	2.000
22	19.660	17.658	14.451	12.042	10.201	8.772	7.645	6.743	6.359	6.011	5.410	4.909	4.488	4.130	3.970	3.822	3.556	3.323	2.853	2.498	2.222	2.000
23	20.456	18.292	14.857	12.303	10.371	8.883	7.718	6.792	6.399	6.044	5.432	4.925	4.499	4.137	3.976	3.827	3.559	3.325	2.854	2.499	2.222	2.000
24	21.243	18.914	15.247	12.550	10.529	8.985	7.784	6.835	6.434	6.073	5.451	4.937	4.507	4.143	3.981	3.831	3.562	3.327	2.855	2.499	2.222	2.000
25	22.023	19.523	15.622	12.783	10.675	9.077	7.843	6.873	6.464	6.097	5.467	4.948	4.514	4.147	3.985	3.834	3.564	3.329	2.856	2.499	2.222	2.000
26	22.795	20.121	15.983	13.003	10.810	9.161	7.896	6.906	6.491	6.118	5.480	4.956	4.520	4.151	3.988	3.837	3.566	3.330	2.856	2.500	2.222	2.000
27	23.560	20.707	16.330	13.211	10.935	9.237	7.943	6.935	6.514	6.136	5.492	4.964	4.524	4.154	3.990	3.839	3.567	3.331	2.856	2.500	2.222	2.000
28	24.316	21.281	16.663	13.406	11.051	9.307	7.984	6.961	6.534	6.152	5.502	4.970	4.528	4.157	3.992	3.840	3.568	3.331	2.857	2.500	2.222	2.000
29	25.066	21.844	16.984	13.591	11.158	9.370	8.022	6.983	6.551	6.166	5.510	4.975	4.531	4.159	3.994	3.841	3.569	3.332	2.857	2.500	2.222	2.000
30	25.808	22.396	17.292	13.765	11.258	9.427	8.055	7.003	6.566	6.177	5.517	4.979	4.534	4.160	3.995	3.842	3.569	3.332	2.857	2.500	2.222	2.000
40	32.835	27.355	19.793	15.046	11.925	9.779	8.244	7.105	6.642	6.234	5.548	4.997	4.544	4.166	3.999	3.846	3.571	3.333	2.857	2.500	2.222	2.000
50	39.196	31.424	21.482	15.762	12.234	9.915	8.304	7.133	6.661	6.246	5.554	4.999	4.545	4.167	4.000	3.846	3.571	3.333	2.857	2.500	2.222	2.000

From Robert N. Anthony and James S. Reece, Accounting: Text and Cases, 7th ed. Homewood, Ill.: Richard D. Irwin, Inc., 1983, p. 962. Reprinted with permission of the Harvard Business School.

Appendix C. Future Values of an Annuity of $1

	2%	3%	4%	5%	6%	8%	10%
1......	1.0000	1.0000	1.0000	1.0000	1.0000	1.0000	1.0000
2......	2.0200	2.0300	2.0400	2.0500	2.0600	2.0800	2.1000
3......	3.0604	3.0909	3.1216	3.1525	3.1836	3.2464	3.3100
4......	4.1216	4.1836	4.2465	4.3101	4.3746	4.5061	4.6410
5......	5.2040	5.3091	5.4163	5.5256	5.6371	5.8666	6.1051
6......	6.3081	6.4684	6.6330	6.8019	6.9753	7.3359	7.7156
7......	7.4343	7.6625	7.8983	8.1420	8.3938	8.9228	9.4872
8......	8.5830	8.8923	9.2142	9.5491	9.8975	10.6366	11.4360
9......	9.7546	10.1591	10.5828	11.0266	11.4913	12.4876	13.5796
10......	10.9497	11.4639	12.0061	12.5779	13.1808	14.4866	15.9376
11......	12.1687	12.8078	13.4864	14.2068	14.9716	16.6455	18.5314
12......	13.4121	14.1920	15.0258	15.9171	16.8699	18.9771	21.3846
13......	14.6803	15.6178	16.6268	17.7130	18.8821	21.4953	24.5231
14......	15.9739	17.0863	18.2919	19.5986	21.0151	24.2149	27.9755
15......	17.2934	18.5989	20.0236	21.5786	23.2760	27.1521	31.7731
16......	18.6393	20.1569	21.8245	23.6575	25.6725	30.3243	35.9503
17......	20.0121	21.7616	23.6975	25.8404	28.2129	33.7502	40.5456
18......	21.4123	23.4144	25.6454	28.1324	30.9057	37.4502	45.6001
19......	22.8406	25.1169	27.6712	30.5390	33.7600	41.4463	51.1601
20......	24.2974	26.8704	29.7781	33.0660	36.7856	45.7620	57.2761
22......	27.2990	30.5368	34.2480	38.5052	43.3923	55.4568	71.4041
24......	30.4219	34.4265	39.0826	44.5020	50.8156	66.7648	88.4989
26......	33.6709	38.5530	44.3117	51.1135	59.1564	79.9544	109.1835
28......	37.0512	42.9309	49.9676	58.4026	68.5281	95.3388	134.2119
30......	40.5681	47.5754	56.0849	66.4388	79.0582	113.2832	164.4962
32......	44.2270	52.5028	62.7015	75.2988	90.8898	134.2135	201.1402
34......	48.0338	57.7302	69.8579	85.0670	104.1838	158.6267	245.4796
36......	51.9944	63.2759	77.5983	95.8363	119.1209	187.1021	299.1302
38......	56.1149	69.1594	85.9703	107.7095	135.9042	220.3159	364.0475
40......	60.4020	75.4013	95.0255	120.7998	154.7620	259.0565	442.5974
42......	64.8622	82.0232	104.8196	135.2318	175.9505	304.2435	537.6428
44......	69.5027	89.0484	115.4129	151.1430	199.7580	356.9496	652.6478
46......	74.3306	96.5015	126.8706	168.6852	226.5081	418.4261	791.8039
48......	79.3535	104.4084	139.2632	188.0254	256.5645	490.1322	960.1827
50......	84.5794	112.7969	152.6671	209.3480	290.3359	573.7702	1163.9209
60......	114.0515	163.0534	237.9907	353.5837	533.1282	1253.2133	3034.8470

Appendix D. The Effect of Age on Pension Cost

Interest rate		2%	4%	6%	8%	10%
Lump sum needed at age 65 to provide $100.00 per month		$15,418.80	$13,341.60	$11,654.40	$10,270.80	$9,127.20
Current age	Years until age 65	Yearly set-aside needed to obtain desired lump sum				
60	5	$ 2,962.87	$ 2,463.23	$ 2,067.45	$ 1,750.72	$1,495.01
55	10	1,408.19	1,111.24	884.20	708.99	572.68
50	15	891.10	666.29	500.70	378.27	287.26
45	20	634.59	448.03	316.82	224.44	159.35
40	25	481.14	319.96	211.94	168.06	118.16
35	30	380.07	237.88	147.42	90.66	55.49
30	35	308.29	180.96	104.37	59.41	33.52
25	40	255.20	140.40	75.31	39.65	20.62
20	45	214.40	121.14	54.68	26.49	12.63

Appendix E. Mortality Table—Males

Age	Number Living	Live to 65	Die Before 65	Life Expectancy for Age Group
10	1,000,000	77.2%	22.8%	66
11	999,517	77.2	22.8	65
12	999,025	77.2	22.8	64
13	998,524	77.3	22.7	63
14	998,013	77.3	22.7	62
15	997,490	77.4	22.6	61
16	996,954	77.4	22.6	60
17	996,405	77.5	22.5	59
18	995,840	77.5	22.5	58
19	995,258	77.5	22.5	57
20	994,658	77.6	22.4	56
21	994,037	77.6	22.4	55
22	993,393	77.7	22.3	54
23	992,724	77.7	22.3	54
24	992,927	77.7	22.3	53
25	991,299	77.8	22.2	52
26	990,538	77.9	22.1	51
27	989,740	78.0	22.0	50
28	988,900	78.1	21.9	49
29	988,013	78.2	21.8	48
30	987,077	78.3	21.7	47
31	986,087	78.3	21.7	46
32	985,035	78.3	21.7	45
33	983,916	78.4	21.6	44
34	982,722	78.5	21.5	43
35	981,447	78.6	21.4	42
36	980,082	78.7	21.3	41
37	978,618	78.9	21.1	40
38	977,045	79.0	21.0	39
39	975,352	79.1	20.9	39
40	973,526	79.3	20.7	37
41	971,555	79.4	20.6	36
42	969,308	79.6	20.4	35
43	966,993	79.8	20.2	34
44	964,282	80.0	20.0	33
45	961,208	80.3	19.7	32

Mortality Table—Males—*Cont'd*

Age	Number Living	Live to 65	Die Before 65	Life Expectancy for Age Group
46	957,724	80.6%	19.4%	31
47	953,782	80.9	19.1	30
48	949,340	81.3	18.7	29
49	944,360	81.7	18.3	28
50	938,807	82.1	17.9	27
51	932,651	82.7	17.3	26
52	925,864	83.3	16.7	26
53	918,422	84.0	16.0	25
54	910,303	84.8	15.2	24
55	901,490	85.6	14.4	23
56	891,966	86.5	13.5	22
57	881,716	87.5	12.5	21
58	870,730	88.6	11.4	20
59	858,996	89.8	10.2	20
60	846,504	91.2	8.8	19
61	833,246	92.6	7.4	18
62	819,190	94.2	5.8	17
63	804,282	95.9	4.1	16
64	788,465	97.9	2.1	16
65	771,684	100.0	—	15
66	753,884	—	—	14
67	735,015	—	—	14
68	715,027	—	—	13
69	693,879	—	—	12
70	671,535	—	—	12
71	647,969	—	—	11
72	623,170	—	—	10
73	597,140	—	—	10
74	569,898	—	—	9
75	541,488	—	—	9

Based on 1949 Annuity Mortality Table, without projection. This table was selected for the purpose of illustration. A more current and commonly used table is the 1971 Group Annuity Table.

Appendix F. Pension Costs Adjusted for Mortality and Turnover

(1) Age	(2) Members	(3) Yearly Cost per Employee to Provide $100 Monthly at Age 65	(4) Yearly Cost Taking Account of Interest (2 × 3)	(5) Percent Living Until 65	(6) Yearly Cost Taking Account of Interest and Mortality (4) × (5)	(7) Percent Staying Until 65	(8) Yearly Cost Taking Account of Interest, Mortality, and Turnover (6) × (7)
60	2	$2,067.45	$ 4,134.90	.912	$ 3,771.03	100	$ 3,771.03
55	5	884.20	4,421.00	.856	3,784.38	100	3,784.38
50	0	0	0	.821	0	100	0
45	10	316.82	3,168.20	.803	2,544.06	95	2,413.86
40	4	211.94	847.76	.793	672.27	95	638.66
35	0	0	0	.786	0	90	0
30	20	104.37	2,087.40	.783	1,634.43	90	1,470.99
25	0	0	0	.788	0	85	0
20	0	0	0	.776	0	75	0
Total	41		$14,659.26		$12,406.17		$12,031.92

Appendix G. Pension Summary Analysis

Date Completed: _____

Local _____ Contract Exp. Date: _____

Present Language	Contract Demands/Comments
I. *Participation:*	
II. *Accrual of Service for Benefit Purposes:*	
III. *Accrual of Service for Vesting Purposes:*	
IV. *Break-in-Service Rule:*	
V. *Normal Retirement:* A. Age B. Normal Retirement Benefit Formula C. Service After Age 65	
VI. *Early Retirement:* A. Eligibility B. Benefit	

Pension Summary Analysis—*Cont'd*

VII. *Disability Retirement:* 　　A. Eligibility 　　B. Benefit	
VIII. *Benefit Payment Options:*	
IX. *Preretirement Surviving Spouse:* 　　A. Eligibility 　　B. Benefit	
X. *Funding:*	
XI. *Investment:*	
XII. *Reports to the Union:*	
XIII. *Administration:*	
XIV. *Other:*	

Appendix H. Letter Requesting Pension Information Held by Company

Mythical Plating Co.
1852 Beecher Way
Eliza, Ohio 43078

Dear _____:

In order to intelligently prepare for negotiations regarding the Local 3520 Pension Plan, it is necessary that we be provided the following information:

1. Active pension plan participants categorized by age, seniority and credited service (vesting and benefit).
2. Retired participants categorized by date of retirement, age, credited service at retirement, amount and type of monthly benefit.
3. Annual company contributions to the pension plan with schedule of dates and level of contributions.
4. The three most recent actuarial evaluations.
5. The three latest Department of Labor 5500 Forms.
6. The three latest trustee reports. If the plan is carried by an insurance company, then the latest three annual reports from the insurance company.
7. A statement indicating any major changes in fund accounting procedures or assumptions which have occurred during the last three years.

If there is any difficulty providing the above listed information, please contact me so that we can discuss alternative sources and formats.

Sincerely,

_____

Appendix I. Actuarial Assumptions and Cost Method

Valuation Date: January 1, 1984.

Retirement Age: The later of age 63 or completion of 10 years of service but no later than age 70.

Mortality Rates:
Nondisabled employees The 1971 Group Annuity Mortality Table.
Disabled employees The ultimate portion of the 1956 Railroad Board Disabled Annuitants Mortality Table.

Withdrawal Rates:
Termination See Table A.
Disability See Table B.

Investment Return: Eight percent per year compounded annually.

Expenses: Normal cost is increased by estimated noninvestment expenses equal to $20,000 for 1984.

Valuation of Assets: The expected value each year is determined by accumulating the prior year's valuation assets plus actual contributions less payments, using the interest rate that is used to value plan liabilities. Preliminary valuation assets are then determined to be the expected asset value plus (or minus) 20% of the excess (or deficit) of the market value over the expected asset value. The final valuation asset amount is equal to the preliminary asset value, subject to the condition that it shall not be less than 80% of the market value of plan assets, nor more than 120% of the market value of plan assets.

Spouse's Option: 90% of males and 70% of females are assumed eligible for a spouse's benefit. Males are assumed to be three years older than their spouses.

Actuarial Cost Method: Entry Age (Level Amount) Cost Method.
(Ongoing Valuation)

Actuarial Assumptions and Cost Method—*Cont'd*

Table A. Nondisabled Withdrawals per 1,000 Participants

Present Age	Male	Female	Present Age	Male	Female
15	300	351	35	50	74
16	278	330	36	48	71
17	256	309	37	46	68
18	234	288	38	43	65
19	212	267	39	41	62
20	190	246	40	39	59
21	168	225	41	37	56
22	146	204	42	35	52
23	132	183	43	33	49
24	118	162	44	31	46
25	104	141	45	28	43
26	90	120	46	26	39
27	76	99	47	24	36
28	72	96	48	22	33
29	68	93	49	19	29
30	64	90	50	17	25
31	60	87	51	14	29
32	56	83	52	11	17
33	54	80	53	9	12
34	52	77	54	6	8
			55	3	4
			56	1	1
			57 +	0	0

Actuarial Assumptions and Cost Method—*Cont'd*

Table B. Disabilities per 1,000 Participants

Present Age	Male	Female	Present Age	Male	Female
15	.4	.4	40	1.1	1.8
16	.4	.4	41	1.2	2.1
17	.4	.4	42	1.4	2.4
18	.4	.4	43	1.7	2.7
19	.4	.4	44	1.9	3.0
20	.4	.4	45	2.2	3.4
21	.4	.4	46	2.5	3.7
22	.4	.4	47	2.9	4.1
23	.4	.4	48	3.4	4.6
24	.4	.4	49	4.0	5.1
25	.4	.4	50	4.6	5.6
26	.4	.5	51	5.5	6.2
27	.4	.5	52	6.5	6.8
28	.1	.5	53	7.5	7.5
29	.4	.5	54	8.5	8.2
30	.4	.6	55	9.6	8.9
31	.4	.6	56	10.7	9.6
32	.4	.7	57	12.0	10.4
33	.4	.8	58	13.3	11.2
34	.5	.9	59	14.7	11.9
35	.5	1.0	60	16.1	12.7
36	.6	1.1	61	17.1	13.4
37	.7	1.3	62	19.4	14.1
38	.8	1.4	63	21.1	14.7
39	.9	1.6	64	22.9	15.2

Appendix J

Form **5500** Department of the Treasury Internal Revenue Service Department of Labor Pension and Welfare Benefit Programs Pension Benefit Guaranty Corporation	**Annual Return/Report of Employee Benefit Plan** **(With 100 or more participants)** This form is required to be filed under sections 104 and 4065 of the Employee Retirement Income Security Act of 1974 and sections 6057(b) and 6058(a) of the Internal Revenue Code, referred to as the Code. ▶ For Paperwork Reduction Act Notice, see page 1 of the instructions.	OMB No. 1210-0016 19**84** This Form is Open to Public Inspection

For the calendar plan year 1984 or fiscal plan year beginning _____ , 1984, and ending _____ , 19 ___

Type or print in ink all entries on the form, schedules, and attachments. If an item does not apply, enter "N/A." File the originals.

This return/report is: *(i)* ☐ the return/report filed for the plan's first year; *(ii)* ☐ an amended return/report; or
(iii) ☐ the final return/report filed for the plan.

▶ Caution: A penalty of $25 a day for the late or incomplete filing of this return/report will be assessed unless reasonable cause is established—see General Instruction F.
▶ Welfare benefit plans with 100 or more participants, complete only items 1 through 11, 13 through 16 and item 22.
▶ Keogh (H.R. 10) plans must check the box in item 5(a)(iii).
▶ If you have been granted an extension of time to file this form, you must attach a copy of the approved extension to this form.

Use IRS label. Other- wise, please print or type.	**1 (a)** Name of plan sponsor (employer if for a single employer plan)	**1 (b)** Employer identification number
	Address (number and street)	**1 (c)** Telephone number of sponsor ( )
	City or town, State and ZIP code	**1 (d)** If plan year changed since last return/report, check here. . ▶ ☐
2 (a) Name of plan administrator (if same as plan sponsor enter "Same")		**1 (e)** Business code number ▶
	Address (number and street)	**2 (b)** Administrator's employer identification no.
	City or town, State and ZIP code	**2 (c)** Telephone number of administrator ( )

3 Is the name, address and identification number of the plan sponsor and/or plan administrator the same as they appeared on the last
return/report filed for this plan? ☐ Yes ☐ No. If "No," enter the information from the last return/report in (a) and/or (b).
(a) Sponsor ▶_____EIN _____
(b) Administrator ▶_____EIN _____
(c) If (a) indicates a change in the sponsor's name and EIN, is this a change in sponsorship only? (See specific instructions for
definition of sponsorship.) ☐ Yes ☐ No

4 Check appropriate box to indicate the type of plan entity (check only one box):
(a) ☐ Single-employer plan **(c)** ☐ Multiemployer plan **(e)** ☐ Multiple-employer plan (other)
(b) ☐ Plan of controlled group of corporations **(d)** ☐ Multiple-employer-collectively- **(f)** ☐ Group insurance arrangement
or common control employers bargained plan (of welfare plans)

5 (a) *(i)* Name of plan ▶	**5 (b)** Effective date of plan
(ii) ☐ Check if name of plan changed since last return/report *(iii)* ☐ Check this box if this is a Keogh (H.R. 10) plan.	**5 (c)** Enter three-digit plan number ▶

6 Check at least one item in (a) or (b) and applicable items in (c):
(a) Welfare benefit plan (Plan numbers 501 through 999): *(i)* ☐ Health insurance *(ii)* ☐ Life insurance
(iii) ☐ Supplemental unemployment *(iv)* ☐ Other (specify) ▶ _____
(b) Pension benefit plan (Plan numbers 001 through 500):
(i) Defined benefit plan—(Indicate type of defined benefit plan below):
(A) ☐ Fixed benefit (B) ☐ Unit benefit (C) ☐ Flat benefit (D) ☐ Other (specify) ▶ _____

(ii) Defined contribution plan—(indicate type of defined contribution plan below):
(A) ☐ Profit-sharing (B) ☐ Stock bonus (C) ☐ Target benefit (D) ☐ Other money purchase
(E) ☐ Other (specify) _____
(iii) ☐ Defined benefit plan with benefits based partly on balance of separate account of participant (Code section 414(k))
(iv) ☐ Annuity arrangement of a certain exempt organization (Code section 403(b)(1))
(v) ☐ Custodial account for regulated investment company stock (Code section 403(b)(7))
(vi) ☐ Pension plan utilizing individual retirement accounts or annuities (described in Code section 408) as the sole funding vehicle
for providing benefits
(vii) ☐ Other (specify) ▶

Under penalties of perjury and other penalties set forth in the instructions, I declare that I have examined this return/report, including accompanying schedules and statements, and to the best of my knowledge and belief, it is true, correct, and complete.

Date ▶ _____ Signature of employer/plan sponsor ▶ _____

Date ▶ _____ Signature of plan administrator ▶ _____

Form 5500 (1984) Page **2**

6 (c) Other plan features: *(i)* ☐ Thrift-savings *(ii)* ☐ Participant-directed account plan
    (iii) ☐ Pension plan maintained outside the United States *(iv)* ☐ Master trust (see instructions) ▶----------------

	Yes	No
(d) Single-employer plans enter the tax year end of the employer in which this plan year ends . . ▶ Month ____ Day ____ Year ____		
(e) Is this a pension plan of an affiliated service group?		
(f) Does this plan contain a cash or deferred arrangement described in Code section 401(k)?		

7 Number of participants as of the end of the plan year (welfare plans complete only (a)(iv), (b), (c) and (d)):
    (a) Active participants: *(i)* Number fully vested . . . .
                (ii) Number partially vested . . . .
                (iii) Number nonvested . . . .
                (iv) Total . . . .
    (b) Retired or separated participants receiving benefits . . . .
    (c) Retired or separated participants entitled to future benefits . . . .
    (d) Subtotal (add (a)(iv), (b) and (c)) . . . .
    (e) Deceased participants whose beneficiaries are receiving or are entitled to receive benefits . . . . .
    (f) Total (add (d) and (e)) . . . .

	Yes	No
(g) *(i)* Was any participant(s) separated from service with a deferred vested benefit for which a Schedule SSA (Form 5500) is required to be attached to this form?		
(ii) If "Yes," enter the number of separated participants required to be reported ▶		

8 Plan amendment information (welfare plans do not complete (b)(ii)):

	Yes	No
(a) Was any amendment to this plan adopted in this plan year?		
(b) If "Yes," *(i)* And if any amendments have resulted in a change in the information contained in a summary plan description or previously furnished summary description of modifications—		
(A) Have summary descriptions of the change(s) been sent to participants?		
(B) Have summary descriptions of the change(s) been filed with DOL?		
(ii) Does any amendment result in the reduction of the accrued benefit of any participant under the plan? .		
(c) Enter the date the most recent amendment was adopted . . . ▶ Month ____ Day ____ Year ____		
(d) *(i)* Has a summary plan description been filed with DOL for this plan?		
(ii) If (i) is "Yes," what was the employer identification number and the plan number used to identify it?		
Employer identification number ▶ Plan number ▶		

9 Plan termination information (welfare plans complete only (a), (b), (c) and (f)):

	Yes	No
(a) Was this plan terminated during this plan year or any prior plan year? . . . . If "Yes," enter year ▶ _____		
(b) Were all plan assets either distributed to participants or beneficiaries, transferred to another plan, or brought under the control of PBGC?		
(c) Was a resolution to terminate this plan adopted during this plan year or any prior plan year?		
(d) If (a) or (c) is "Yes," have you received a favorable determination letter from IRS for the termination?		
(e) If (d) is "No," has a determination letter been requested from IRS?		
(f) If (a) or (c) is "Yes," have participants and beneficiaries been notified of the termination or the proposed termination?		
(g) If (a) is "Yes," and the plan is covered by PBGC, is the plan continuing to file a PBGC Form 1 and pay premiums until the end of the plan year in which assets are distributed or brought under the control of PBGC?		

10 (a) In this plan year, was this plan merged or consolidated into another plan, or were assets or liabilities transferred to another plan? . . . .
    If "Yes," identify other plan(s):

	(c) Employer identification number(s)	**(d)** Plan number(s)
(b) Name of plan(s) ▶ --------------------------		

(e) Has Form 5310 been filed? . . . . ☐ Yes ☐ No

11 Indicate funding arrangement: **(a)** ☐ Trust (benefits provided in whole from trust funds)
    (b) ☐ Trust or arrangement providing benefits partially through insurance and/or annuity contracts
    (c) ☐ Trust or arrangement providing benefits exclusively through insurance and/or annuity contracts
    (d) ☐ Custodial account described in Code section 401(f) and not included in (c) above
    (e) ☐ Other (specify) ▶ ---
    (f) If (b) or (c) is checked, enter the number of Schedules A (Form 5500) which are attached . . . . ▶

12 (a) Has the plan used the services of a contract administrator (see instructions)? . . . . ☐ Yes ☐ No
    If "Yes," you must complete line (1) of the schedule below.
    (b) Did any other person who rendered services to the plan receive, directly or indirectly, compensation from the plan in the plan year? ☐ Yes ☐ No
    If "Yes," furnish the following information starting on line (2):

a. Name	b. Employer identification number (see instructions)	c. Official plan position	d. Relationship to employer, employee organization, or person known to be a party-in-interest	e. Gross salary or allowances paid by plan	f. Fees and commissions paid by plan	g. Nature of service code (see instructions)
(1)		Contract admin.				13
(2)						
(3)						

Form 5500 (1984)   Page **3**

13 Plan assets and liabilities at the beginning and the end of the plan year (list all assets and liabilities at current value). A fully insured welfare plan or a pension plan with no trust and which is funded entirely by allocated insurance contracts which fully guarantee the amount of benefit payments should check the box and not complete the rest of this item ▶ . . . . □

Note: *Include all plan assets and liabilities of a trust or separately maintained fund. (If more than one trust/fund, report on a combined basis.) Include all insurance values except for the value of that portion of an allocated insurance contract which fully guarantees the amount of benefit payments. Round off amounts to the nearest dollar. Trusts with no assets at the beginning and the end of the plan year enter zero on line 13(h).*

Assets	a. Beginning of year	b. End of year
(a) Cash: *(i)* On hand		
(ii) In bank: (A) Certificate of deposit		
(B) Other interest bearing		
(C) Noninterest bearing		
(iii) Total cash (add (i) and (ii))		
(b) Receivables: *(i)* Employer contributions		
(ii) Employee contributions		
(iii) Other		
(iv) Reserve for doubtful accounts		
(v) Net receivables (subtract (iv) from the total of (i),(ii) and (iii))		
(c) General investments other than party-in-interest investments:		
(i) U.S. Government securities (A) Long term		
(B) Short term		
(ii) State and municipal securities		
(iii) Corporate debt instruments: (A) Long term		
(B) Short term		
(iv) Corporate stocks: (A) Preferred		
(B) Common		
(v) Shares of a registered investment company		
(vi) Real estate		
(vii) Mortgages		
(viii) Loans other than mortgages		
(ix) Value of interest in pooled fund(s)		
(x) Value of interest in master trust		
(xi) Other investments		
(xii) Total general investments (add (i) through (xi))		
(d) Party-in-interest investments:		
(i) Corporate debt instruments		
(ii) Corporate stocks: (A) Preferred		
(B) Common		
(iii) Real estate		
(iv) Mortgages		
(v) Loans other than mortgages		
(vi) Other investments		
(vii) Total party-in-interest investments (add (i) through (vi))		
(e) Buildings and other depreciable property used in plan operation		
(f) Value of unallocated insurance contracts (other than pooled separate accounts):		
(i) Separate accounts		
(ii) Other		
(iii) Total (add (i) and (ii))		
(g) Other assets		
(h) Total assets (add (a)(iii), (b)(v), (c)(xii), (d)(vii), (e), (f)(iii) and (g))		
Liabilities		
(i) Payables: *(i)* Plan claims		
(ii) Other payables		
(iii) Total payables (add (i) and (ii))		
(j) Acquisition indebtedness		
(k) Other liabilities		
(l) Total liabilities (add (i), (j), and (k))		
(m) Net assets (subtract (l) from (h))		
(n) During the plan year what were the:		
(i) Total costs of acquisitions for common stock?		
(ii) Total proceeds from dispositions of common stock?		

Form 5500 (1984)   Page **4**

14 Plan income, expenses and changes in net assets for the plan year.

Note: *Include all income and expenses of a trust(s) or separately maintained fund(s) including any payments made for allocated insurance contracts. Round off amounts to nearest dollar.*

Income	a. Amount	b. Total
(a) Contributions received or receivable in cash from—		
(i) Employer(s) (including contributions on behalf of self-employed individuals)		
(ii) Employees		
(iii) Others		
(b) Noncash contributions (specify nature and by whom made) ▶		
(c) Total contributions (add total of (a)(iii) and (b))		
(d) Earnings from investments—		
(i) Interest		
(ii) Dividends		
(iii) Rents		
(iv) Royalties		
(e) Net realized gain (loss) on sale or exchange of assets—		
(i) Aggregate proceeds		
(ii) Aggregate costs		
(f) Other income (specify) ▶		
(g) Total income (add (c) through (f))		

Expenses	a. Amount	b. Total
(h) Distribution of benefits and payments to provide benefits—		
(i) Directly to participants or their beneficiaries		
(ii) To insurance carrier or similar organization for provision of benefits		
(iii) To other organizations or individuals providing welfare benefits		
(i) Interest expense		
(j) Administrative expenses—		
(i) Salaries and allowances		
(ii) Fees and commissions		
(iii) Insurance premiums for Pension Benefit Guaranty Corporation		
(iv) Insurance premiums for fiduciary insurance other than bonding		
(v) Other administrative expenses		
(k) Other expenses (specify) ▶		
(l) Total expenses (add (h) through (k))		
(m) Net income (expenses) (subtract (l) from (g))		

	a. Amount	b. Total
(n) Changes in net assets —		
(i) Unrealized appreciation (depreciation) of assets		
(ii) Net investment gain (or loss) from all master trust investment accounts		
(iii) Other changes (specify) ▶		
(o) Net increase (decrease) in net assets for the year (add (m) and (n))		
(p) Net assets at beginning of year (line 13(m), column a)		
(q) Net assets at end of year (add (o) and (p)) (equals line 13(m), column b)		

15 All plans complete (a). Plans funded with insurance policies or annuity contracts also complete (b) and (c):

	Yes	No
(a) Since the end of the plan year covered by the last return/report has there been a termination in the appointment of any trustee, accountant, insurance carrier, enrolled actuary, administrator, investment manager or custodian?		

If "Yes," explain and include the name, position, address and telephone number of the person whose appointment has been terminated ▶

(b) Have any insurance policies or annuities been replaced during this plan year?

If "Yes," explain the reason for the replacement ▶

(c) At any time during the plan year was the plan funded with:

(i) ☐ Individual policies or annuities, *(ii)* ☐ Group policies or annuities, or *(iii)* ☐ Both.

Form 5500 (1984)   Page **5**

		Yes	No

16 Bonding:

(a) Was the plan insured by a fidelity bond against losses through fraud or dishonesty? . . . .
  If "Yes," complete (b) through (f); if "No," only complete (g).

(b) Indicate the number of plans covered by this bond ▶ . . . .

(c) Enter the maximum amount of loss recoverable ▶ . . . .

(d) Enter the name of the surety company ▶ . . . .
. . . .

(e) Does the plan, or a known party-in-interest with respect to the plan, have any control or significant financial interest,
  direct or indirect, in the surety company or its agents or brokers? . . . .

(f) In the current plan year was any loss to the plan caused by the fraud or dishonesty of any plan official or employee of
  the plan or of other person handling funds of the plan? . . . .
  If "Yes," see Specific Instructions.

(g) If the plan is not insured by a fidelity bond, explain why not ▶ . . . .
. . . .

17 Information about employees of employer at end of the plan year.

(a) Does the plan satisfy the percentage tests of Code section 410(b)(1)(A)? If "No," complete only (b) below and see
  Specific Instructions . . . .

(b) Total number of employees . . . .

(c) Number of employees excluded under the plan because of:

  (i) Minimum age or years of service . . . .

  (ii) Employees on whose behalf retirement benefits were the subject of collective bargaining . . . .

  (iii) Nonresident aliens who receive no earned income from United States sources . . . .

  (iv) Total excluded (add (i), (ii) and (iii)) . . . .

(d) Total number of employees not excluded (subtract (c)(iv) from (b)) . . . .

(e) Employees ineligible (specify reason) ▶ . . . .

(f) Employees eligible to participate (subtract (e) from (d)) . . . .

(g) Employees eligible but not participating . . . .

(h) Employees participating (subtract (g) from (f)) . . . .

18 Is this plan an adoption of any of the plans below? (If "Yes," check appropriate box and enter IRS serial number): | Yes | No

(a) ☐ Master/prototype, (b) ☐ Field prototype, (c) ☐ Pattern, (d) ☐ Model plan, or (e) ☐ Bond purchase plan . . .
  Enter the four or eight-digit IRS serial number (see instructions) ▶

19 (a) Is it intended that this plan qualify under Code section 401(a) or 405? . . . .

(b) Have you requested or received a determination letter from the IRS for this plan? . . . .

(c) Is this a plan with Employee Stock Ownership Plan features? . . . .

  (i) If "Yes," was a current appraisal of the value of the stock made immediately before any contribution of stock
    or the purchase of the stock by the trust for the plan year covered by this return/report? . . . .

  (ii) If (i) is "Yes," was the appraisal made by an unrelated third party? . . . .

20 (a) If plan is integrated, check appropriate box:

  (i) ☐ Social security   (ii) ☐ Railroad retirement   (iii) ☐ Other

(b) Does the employer/sponsor listed in item 1(a) of this form maintain other qualified pension benefit plans? . . . .
  If "Yes," list the number of plans including this plan ▶

21 (a) If this is a defined benefit plan, is it subject to the minimum funding standards for this plan year? . . . .
  If "Yes," attach Schedule B (Form 5500).

(b) If this is a defined contribution plan, i.e., money purchase or target benefit, is it subject to the minimum funding
  standards? (If a waiver was granted, see instructions.) . . . .
  If "Yes," complete (i), (ii) and (iii) below:

  (i) Amount of employer contribution required for the plan year under Code section 412 . . . .

  (ii) Amount of contribution paid by the employer for the plan year . . . .
    Enter date of last payment by employer . . . . . ▶ Month _____ Day _____ Year _____

  (iii) If (i) is greater than (ii), subtract (ii) from (i) and enter the funding deficiency here; otherwise enter
    zero. (If you have a funding deficiency, file Form 5330.) . . . .

22 Answer questions (a), (b), and (c) relating to the plan year. If (a)(i), (ii), (iii), (iv) or (v) is checked "Yes," schedules of | Yes | No
those items in the format set forth in the instructions are required to be attached to this form.

(a) (i) Did the plan have assets held for investment? . . . .

  (ii) Did any non-exempt transaction involving plan assets involve a party known to be a party-in-interest? . . . .

  (iii) Were any loans by the plan or fixed income obligations due the plan in default as of the close of the plan year
    or classified during the year as uncollectable? . . . .

Form 5500 (1984)

22 *(Continued)*

	Yes	No
(iv) Were any leases to which the plan was a party in default or classified during the year as uncollectable?		
(v) Were any plan transactions or series of transactions in excess of 3% of the current value of plan assets? . . .		

(b) The accountant's opinion is *(i)* ☐ Required, or *(ii)* ☐ Not required

(c) If the accountant's opinion is required, attach it to this form and check the appropriate box. This opinion is:

    (i) ☐ Unqualified

    (ii) ☐ Qualified

    (iii) ☐ Adverse

    (iv) ☐ Other (explain) ▶

23 (a) Is the plan covered under the Pension Benefit Guaranty Corporation termination insurance program? . . . . ☐ **Yes** ☐ **No** ☐ **Not determined**

(b) If (a) is "Yes," or "Not determined," enter the employer identification number and the plan number used to identify it.

Employer identification number ▶   Plan number ▶

	Yes	No
24 (a) Is this plan a top-heavy plan within the meaning of Code section 416 for this plan year?		
(b) If (a) is "Yes," complete (i), (ii) and (iii) below:		
(i) Has the plan complied with the vesting requirements of Code section 416(b)?		
(ii) Has the plan complied with the minimum benefit requirements of Code section 416(c)?		
(iii) Has the plan complied with the limitation on compensation of Code section 416(d)?		
25 Have any individuals performed services as a leased employee for this employer or for any other employer who is aggregated with this employer under section 414(b), (c), or (m)? . . . . If "Yes," see instructions for completing item 17.		

✿ U.S. GOVERNMENT PRINTING OFFICE: 1985-423-261   E.I.   43-0787287

SCHEDULE A (Form 5500) Department of the Treasury Internal Revenue Service Department of Labor Pension and Welfare Benefit Programs Pension Benefit Guaranty Corporation	**Insurance Information** This schedule is required to be filed under section 104 of the Employee Retirement Income Security Act of 1974. ▶ File as an Attachment to Forms 5500, 5500-C, or 5500-R	OMB No. 1210-0016 **1984** This Form Is Open to Public Inspection

For calendar year 1984 or fiscal plan year beginning _____ , 1984 and ending _____ , 19 ____

▶ Part I must be completed for all plans required to file this schedule.
▶ Part II must be completed for all insured pension plans.
▶ Part III must be completed for all insured welfare plans.

▶ Enter master trust name in place of "sponsor" and specify investment account in place of "plan" if filing for a master trust.

Name of plan sponsor as shown on line 1(a) of Form 5500, 5500-C, or 5500-R	Employer identification number

Name of plan	Enter three digit plan number ▶

Part I   Summary of All Insurance Contracts Included in Parts II and III
Group all contracts in the same manner as in Parts II and III.

1 Check appropriate box: (a) ☐ Welfare plan (b) ☐ Pension plan (c) ☐ Combination pension and welfare plan

2 Coverage: (a) Name of insurance carrier	(b) Contract or identification number	(c) Approximate number of persons covered at end of policy or contract year	Policy or contract year	
			(d) From	(e) To

3 Insurance fees and commissions paid to agents and brokers:		(c) Amount of commissions paid	(d) Fees paid	
(a) Contract or identification number	(b) Name and address of the agents or brokers to whom commissions or fees were paid		Amount	Purpose
Total				

4 Premiums due and unpaid at end of the plan year ▶ $ _____ , contract or identification number ▶

Part II   Insured Pension Plans Provide information for each contract on a separate Part II. Where individual contracts are provided, the entire group of such individual contracts with each carrier may be treated as a unit for purposes of this report.

▶ Contract or identification number ▶

5 Contracts with allocated funds, for example, individual policies or group deferred annuity contracts:
 (a) State the basis of premium rates ▶ _____
 (b) Total premiums paid to carrier . . . .
 (c) If the carrier, service or other organization incurred any specific costs in connection with the acquisition or retention of the contract or policy, other than reported in 3 above, enter amount . . . .
    Specify nature of costs ▶

6 Contracts with unallocated funds, for example, deposit administration or immediate participation guarantee contracts. Do not include portions of these contracts maintained in separate accounts:
 (a) Balance at the end of the previous policy year . . . .
 (b) Additions: (i) Contributions deposited during year . . . .
   (ii) Dividends and credits . . . .
   (iii) Interest credited during the year . . . .
   (iv) Transferred from separate account . . . .
   (v) Other (specify) ▶ _____
   (vi) Total additions . . . .
 (c) Total of balance and additions, add (a) and (b)(vi) . . . .
 (d) Deductions:
   (i) Disbursed from fund to pay benefits or purchase annuities during year. . . . . .
   (ii) Administration charge made by carrier . . . .
   (iii) Transferred to separate account . . . .
   (iv) Other (specify) ▶ _____
   (v) Total deductions . . . .
 (e) Balance at end of current policy year, subtract (d)(v) from (c) . . . .
7 Separate accounts: Current value of plan's interest in separate accounts at year end . . . .

For Paperwork Reduction Act Notice, see page 1 of the Instructions for Form 5500.   Schedule A (Form 5500) 1984

Schedule A (Form 5500) 1984   Page **2**

Part III   Insured Welfare Plans

Provide information for each contract on a separate Part III. If more than one contract covers the same group of employees of the same employer(s) or members of the same employee organization(s), the information may be combined for reporting purposes if such contracts are experience-rated as a unit. Where individual contracts are provided, the entire group of such individual contracts with each carrier may be treated as a unit for purposes of this report.

8 (a) Contract or identification number	(b) Type of benefit	(c) List gross premium for each contract	(d) Premium rate or subscription charge

9   Experience rated contracts: **(a)** Premiums: *(i)* Amount received . . . .

    (ii)   Increase (decrease) in amount due but unpaid . . . .

    (iii)   Increase (decrease) in unearned premium reserve . . . . .

    (iv)   Premiums earned, add (i) and (ii), and subtract (iii) . . . .

  (b) Benefit charges: *(i)* Claims paid . . . .

    (ii)   Increase (decrease) in claim reserves . . . .

    (iii)   Incurred claims, add (i) and (ii) . . . .

    (iv)   Claims charged . . . .

  (c) Remainder of premium: *(i)* Retention charges (on an accrual basis)—(A) Commissions .

    (B)   Administrative service or other fees . . . .

    (C)   Other specific acquisition costs . . . .

    (C)   Other expenses . . . .

    (E)   Taxes . . . .

    (F)   Charges for risks or contingencies . . . .

    (G)   Other retention charges . . . .

    (H)   Total retention . . . .

    (ii) Dividends or retroactive rate refunds. (These amounts were ☐ paid in cash or ☐ credited.) . .

  (d) Status of policyholder reserves at end of year: *(i)* Amount held to provide benefits after retirement . . . .

    (ii)   Claim reserves . . . .

    (iii)   Other reserves . . . .

  (e) Dividends or retroactive rate refunds due (do not include amount entered in (c)(ii)) . . . .

10   Non experience rated contracts: (a) Total premiums or subscription charges paid to carrier . . . .

  (b) If the carrier, service or other organization incurred any specific costs in connection with the acquisition or retention of the contract or policy, other than reported in 3 above, report amount . . . .

    Specify nature of costs ▶ _____

If additional space is required for any item, attach additional sheets the same size as this form.

General Instructions

This schedule must be attached to Form 5500, 5500-C, or 5500-R for every defined benefit, defined contribution and welfare benefit plan where any benefits under the plan are provided by an insurance company, insurance service or other similar organization.

Exception: Schedule A (Form 5500) is not needed if the plan covers only (1) an individual (or an individual and spouse) who wholly owns a trade or business, whether incorporated or unincorporated, or (2) a partner in a partnership or a partner and spouse.

Plans Participating in Master Trust(s).—For insurance or annuity contracts that are held in a master trust and owned jointly by two or more plans participating in a master trust, a single Schedule A (Form 5500) for each contract must be included in the information relating to the master trust which is filed with DOL. The individual plans need not file the Schedule A (Form 5500) but must treat unallocated funds or any interest in a separate account held in a master trust as part of an investment account for purposes of their annual report. (See the return/report master trust filing instructions.)

Specific Instructions

(References are to the line items on the form.)

Include only contracts with policy or contract years ending with or within the plan year. Data on Schedule A (Form 5500) should be reported only for such policy or contract years. Exception: If the insurance company maintains records on the basis of a plan year rather than policy or contract year, data on Schedule A (Form 5500) may be reported for the plan year.

Include only the contracts issued to the plan for which this return/report is being filed.

2(c).—Since the plan coverage may fluctuate during the year, the number of persons entered should be that which the administrator determines will most reasonably reflect the number covered by the plan at the end of the policy or contract year.

Where contracts covering individual employees are grouped, entries should be determined as of the end of the plan year.

2(d) and (e).—Enter the beginning and ending dates of the policy year for each contract listed under column (b). Where separate contracts covering individual employees are grouped, enter "N/A" in column (d).

3.—All sales commissions are to be reported in column (c) regardless of the identity of the

recipient. Override commissions, salaries, bonuses, etc., paid to a general agent or manager for managing an agency, or for performing other administrative functions, are not to be reported. Fees to be reported in column (d) represent payments by insurance carriers to agents and brokers for items other than commissions (e.g., service fees, consulting fees and finders fees). Fees paid by insurance carriers to persons other than agents and brokers should be reported in Parts II and III on Schedule A (Form 5500) as acquisition costs, administrative charges, etc., as appropriate. For plans with 100 or more participants, fees paid by employee benefit plans to agents, brokers and other persons are to be reported in item 12, Form 5500.

5(a).—The rate information called for here may be furnished by attachment of appropriate schedules of current rates filed with appropriate State insurance departments or by a statement as to the basis of the rates.

6.—Show deposit fund amounts rather than experience credit records when both are maintained.

8(d).—The rate information called for here may be furnished by attachment of appropriate schedules of current rates or by a statement as to the basis of the rates.

SCHEDULE B (Form 5500) Department of the Treasury Internal Revenue Service Department of Labor Pension and Welfare Benefit Programs Pension Benefit Guaranty Corporation	**Actuarial Information** This schedule is required to be filed under section 104 of the Employee Retirement Income Security Act of 1974, referred to as ERISA, and section 6059(a) of the Internal Revenue Code, referred to as the Code. ► **Attach to Forms 5500, 5500-C, or 5500-R if applicable.**	OMB No. 1210-0016 19**84** This Form Is Open to Public Inspection

For calendar plan year 1984 or fiscal plan year beginning _____, 1984, and ending _____, 19____

► **Please complete every item on this form. If an item does not apply, enter "N/A."**   ► **Round off amounts to nearest dollar.**

► **Caution:** A penalty of $1,000 will be assessed for late filing of this report unless reasonable cause is established.

Name of plan sponsor as shown on line 1(a) of Form 5500, 5500-C, or 5500-R	Employer identification number

Name of plan	Enter three digit plan number ►		Yes	No

1 Has a waiver of a funding deficiency for this plan been approved by the IRS? . . . .

   If "Yes," attach a copy of the IRS approval letter.

2 Is a waived funding deficiency of a prior plan year being amortized in this plan year? . . . .

3 Have any of the periods of amortization for charges described in Code section 412(b)(2)(B) been extended by IRS? . . .

   If "Yes," attach a copy of the IRS approval letter.

4 **(a)** Was the shortfall funding method the basis for this plan year's funding standard account computations? . . . .

   (b) Is this plan a multiemployer plan which is, for this plan year, in reorganization as described in Code section 418 or ERISA section 4241? . . . .

     If "Yes," you are required to attach the information described in the instructions.

5 Has a change in funding method for this plan year been made? . . . .

   If "Yes," attach a copy of the information required to show IRS approval.

6 Operational information:

   (a) Enter most recent actuarial valuation date ► -

   (b) Enter date(s) and amount of contributions received this plan year for prior plan years and not previously reported:

     Date(s) ► - , Amount ►

   (c) Current value of the assets accumulated in the plan as of the beginning of the plan year . . . . .

   (d) Present value of vested benefits as of the beginning of the plan year:

     (i) For retired participants and beneficiaries receiving payments . . . .

     (ii) For other participants . . . .

     (iii) Total . . . .

   (e) Present value of nonvested accrued benefits as of the beginning of the plan year . . . .

   (f) Number of persons covered (included in the most recent actuarial valuation):

     (i) Active participants . . . .

     (ii) Terminated participants with vested benefits . . . .

     (iii) Retired participants and beneficiaries of deceased participants . . . .

7 Contributions made to the plan for the plan year by employer(s) and employees:

(a) Month Day Year	(b) Amount paid by employer	(c) Amount paid by employees	(a) Month Day Year	(b) Amount paid by employer	(c) Amount paid by employees
			Total . . .		

Statement by Enrolled Actuary (see instructions before signing):

   To the best of my knowledge, the information supplied in this schedule and on the accompanying statement, if any, is complete and accurate, and in my opinion the assumptions used in the aggregate (a) are reasonably related to the experience of the plan and to reasonable expectations, and (b) represent my best estimate of anticipated experience under the plan.

-     -

                 Signature of actuary   Date

-     -

            Print or type name of actuary   Enrollment number

-     -

                 Address   Telephone number (including area code)

For Paperwork Reduction Act Notice, see the Instructions for Form 5500   **Schedule B (Form 5500) 1984**

Schedule B (Form 5500) 1984   Page 2

8 Funding standard account and other information:

(a) Accrued liabilities as determined for funding standard account as of (enter date) ▶ _____

(b) Value of assets as determined for funding standard account as of (enter date) ▶ _____

(c) (i) Actuarial gains or (losses) for period ending ▶ _____

(ii) Shortfall gains or (losses) for period ending ▶ _____

(d) Amount of contribution certified by the actuary as necessary to reduce the funding deficiency to zero,
from 9(m) or 10(h) (or the attachment for 4(b) if required) . . . .

9 Funding standard account statement for this plan year ending ▶ _____

Charges to funding standard account:

(a) Prior year funding deficiency, if any . . . .

(b) Employer's normal cost for plan year as of mo. _____ day _____ yr. _____

(c) Amortization charges (outstanding balance as of mo. _____ day _____ yr. _____ ▶ $ _____)

(d) Interest as applicable to the end of the plan year on (a), (b), and (c) . . . . .

(e) Total charge (add (a) through (d)) . . . .

Credits to funding standard account:

(f) Prior year credit balance, if any . . . .

(g) (i) Employer contributions (total from column (b) of item 7) . . . .

(ii) Employer contributions received this plan year for prior plan years and not previously reported . .

(h) Amortization credits (outstanding balance as of mo. _____ day _____ yr. _____ ▶ $ _____)

(i) Interest as applicable to end of plan year on (f), (g), and (h) . . . .

(j) Other (specify) ▶ _____

(k) Total credits (add (f) through (j)) . . . .

Balance:

(l) Credit balance: if (k) is greater than (e), enter the difference . . . . . .

(m) Funding deficiency: if (e) is greater than (k), enter the difference . . . . .

10 Alternative minimum funding standard account (omit if not used):

(a) Was the entry age normal cost method used to determine entries in item 9 above? . . . . . . ☐ Yes ☐ No

If "No," do not complete (b) through (h).

(b) Prior year alternate funding deficiency, if any . . . .

(c) Normal cost . . . .

(d) Excess, if any, of value of accrued benefits over market value of assets . . . .

(e) Interest on (b), (c), and (d) . . . .

(f) Employer contributions (total from column (b) of item 7) . . . .

(g) Interest on (f) . . . .

(h) Funding deficiency: if the sum of (b) through (e) is greater than the sum of (f) and (g), enter difference .

11 Actuarial cost method used as the basis for this plan year's funding standard account computation:

(a) ☐ Attained age normal   (b) ☐ Entry age normal   (c) ☐ Accrued benefit (unit credit)

(d) ☐ Aggregate   (e) ☐ Frozen initial liability (f) ☐ Individual level premium

(g) ☐ Other (specify) ▶

12 Checklist of certain actuarial assumptions:	**A** Used for item 6(d) and (e)— value of accrued benefits				**B** Used for item 8, 9 or 10— funding standard account			
	Pre-retirement		Post-retirement		Pre-retirement		Post-retirement	
(a) Rates specified in insurance or annuity contracts . .	☐ Yes	☐ No	☐ Yes	☐ No	☐ Yes	☐ No	☐ Yes	☐ No
(b) Mortality table code:								
(i) Males								
(ii) Females								
(c) Interest rate	%		%		%		%	
(d) Retirement age . . .	• .							
(e) Expense loading . . .	%		%		%		%	
(f) Annual withdrawal rate:	Male	Female			Male	Female		
(i) Age 25	%	%			%	%		
(ii) Age 40	%	%			%	%		
(iii) Age 55	%	%			%	%		
(g) Ratio of salary at normal retirement to salary at:								
(i) Age 25					%	%		
(ii) Age 40					%	%		
(iii) Age 55					%	%		
(h) Is a statement of actuarial assumptions, actuarial funding method, etc., attached?							☐ Yes	☐ No

Appendix K. DOL 5500 Pension Analysis

Company _____

Location _____

Local Union # _____

U.S. Labor Department File # _____

Plan Year Ending _____
(Month) — (Day)

ITEM	19__	19__	19__	19__	19__
1. Number of employees (P. 2, Sec. 7(a)(iv))					
2. Hours worked (est.)					
3. Employees' contribution (P. 4, Sec. 14(a)(ii))					
4. Cents per hour (employee)[a]					
5. Employer contribution (P. 4, Sec. 14(a)(i))					
6. Cents per hour (employer)[b]					
7. Total contribution[c]					
8. Cents per hour (total)[d]					
9. Number of retirees (P. 2, Sec. 7(b))					
10. Benefits paid out (P. 4, Sec. 14(h)(i))					
11. Average monthly benefit[e]					
12. Assets (start of year) (P. 3, Sec. 13(h) col. a)					
13. Assets (end of year) (P. 3, Sec. 13(h) col. b)					
14. Average assets[f]					

15. Interest income (P. 4, Sec. 14(d)(i))
16. Dividend income (P. 4, Sec. 14(d)(ii))
17. Rents (P. 4, Sec. 14(d)(iii))
18. Royalties (P. 4, Sec. 14(d)(iv))
19. Total investment income[g]
20. Percent return on assets[h]

[a] Cents per hour (employee)

$$\frac{\text{Employees' contribution (3)} \div \text{hours worked (2)}}{\text{number of employees (1)}}$$

[b] Cents per hour (employer)

$$\frac{\text{Employer contribution (5)} \div \text{hours worked (2)}}{\text{number of employees (1)}}$$

[c] Total contribution = employees' contribution (3) + employer contribution (5)

[d] Cents per hour (total) = cents per hour (employee) (4) + cents per hour (employer) (6)

[e] Average monthly benefit = $\dfrac{\text{benefits paid out (10)} \div 12}{\text{number of retirees (9)}}$

[f] Average assets = $\dfrac{\text{assets (start of year) (12)} + \text{assets (end of year) (13)}}{2}$

[g] Total investment income = interest income (15) + dividend income (16) + rents (17) + royalties (18)

[h] Percent return on assets = $\dfrac{\text{total investment income (19)}}{\text{average assets (14)}}$

Appendix L. Computing Fringe Benefits Costs

The well-prepared negotiator must not only know what fringe benefits are needed by the membership, but what these benefits cost. Costing a benefit once you have the relevant data from the employer is a relatively simple task, at most involving some division and a little multiplication. The task is complicated, however, by the fact that the cost of a fringe benefit can be expressed in several ways, three of which are the most common: total annual cost, annual average cost per employee, and average cost per hour worked per employee.

These three cost figures are related. The first is simply the total cost to the employer in a given contract year. The second is the total annual cost divided by the number of employees in the bargaining unit. The third is derived by dividing the average annual cost per employee by the average number of hours worked per year per bargaining unit member.

a. Total Annual Cost = Yearly Cost of Benefit Provision
b. Annual Average Cost per Employee = (a) divided by number of employees
c. Average Cost per Hour Worked per Employee = (b) divided by average number of hours

The following formulas show how to derive the average hourly cost for several benefits common in collective bargaining agreements. For each type of benefit the general formula is given, followed by an example using a hypothetical local union, and a problem that you should complete to make sure you understand how the formula should be used. The fringe benefits are divided into three categories. Insurance-Type Benefits, Paid Leave Time, and Benefits Applying to a Fraction of the Membership.

Insurance-Type Benefits

Initial Abbreviations Appearing Below Stand for:

TAC = Total Annual Cost
AACPE = Annual Average Cost per Employee
ACPHWPE = Average Cost per Hour Worked per Employee

I. Pension

    A. *General Formula:*
        1. TAC = Total employer contribution to pension plan over past year
        2. AACPE = TAC ÷ number of employees.
        3. ACPHWPE = AACPE ÷ average number of hours

B. *Example:*
   Data: employer contribution = $1,000,000
        number of employees = 1,000
        average number of hours = 2,000
   1. TAC = $1,000,000
   2. AACPE = TAC ÷ number of employees = $1,000
   3. ACPHWPE = AACPE ÷ average number of hours = $.50

C. *Problem:*
   The cost of your current pension program is $1,250,000 per year.
   From your discussions with the plan actuary it looks like your
   proposals for improving the current plan will increase the cost of
   the plan by 10%. What is the cost of the improvement in cents per
   hour? Additional information needed: number of employees =
   1,000 and average number of hours = 2,000
   1. TAC = _____
   2. AACPE = TAC ÷ number of employees = _____ ÷

       _____ = _____
   3. ACPHWPE = AACPE ÷ number of hours = _____ ÷

       _____ = _____

II. *Health Insurance*

   A. *General Formula:*
      1. TAC = monthly premium × 12 months × number of employ-
         ees
      2. AACPE = TAC ÷ number of employees
      3. ACPHWPE = AACPE ÷ average number of hours

   B. *Example*
      Data: monthly premium = $75.00
           number of employees = 1,000
           average number of hours = 2,000
      1. TAC = $75.00 × 12 × 1,000 = $900,000
      2. AACPE = $900
      3. ACPHWPE = $.45

   C. *Problem:*
      Within the past few months, a health maintenance organization
      opened in your community. The monthly premium for medical
      and hospital coverage is $71.00 per month for family coverage.
      The monthly premium on your current health insurance program
      is $82.00 per month. Assuming all the cost savings would go into
      increased wages, how much in cents per hour could wages be
      increased if your local switched to the cheaper plan? Additional
      information needed: number of employees = 950 and average
      number of hours = 2,000

Paid Leave Time

I. Holidays

A. General Formula:
1. TAC = total paid holiday hours per employee × number of employees × average hourly wage
2. AACPE = TAC ÷ number of employees
3. ACPHWPE = AACPE ÷ average number of hours worked

B. Example
Data: 10 eight-hour paid holidays
average hourly wage = $5.50
number of employees = 1,000
average number of hours = 2,000
1. TAC = 10 × 8 hours × 1,000 employees × $5.50 = $440,000
2. AACPE = $440,000 ÷ 1,000 = $440
3. ACPHWPE = $440 ÷ 2,000 = $.22

C. Problem:
Your local would like to negotiate one half-day (4 hours) paid leave time per year per member for the purpose of voting in local elections. What is the cost of this proposal in cents per hour? Additional data needed: average hourly wage = $6.32, number of employees = 763, and average number of hours = 1,865

II. Paid Wash-up Time

A. General Formula:
1. TAC = total paid wash-up hours × average hourly wage = minutes off × average number of days worked ÷ 60 minutes × number of employees × average hourly wage
2. AACPE = TAC ÷ number of employees
3. ACPHWPE = AACPE ÷ average number of hours worked

B. Example:
Data: 15 minutes paid wash-up time
average number of days worked = 250
number of employees = 1,000
average number of hours = 2,000
average hourly wage = $5.50
1. TAC = 15 minutes × 250 days ÷ 60 × 1000 × $5.50 = $343,750
2. AACPE = $343,750 ÷ 1,000 = $343.75
3. ACPHWPE = $343.75 ÷ 2,000 = $.172

C. Problem:
Your current contract calls for two 15-minute paid rest periods per day. You would like to propose that each rest period be increased from 15 to 20 minutes. What is the cost of this proposal in cents

per hour? Additional information needed: average hourly wage =
$5.50, average number of days worked = 250, number of employ-
ees = 950, and average number of hours = 2,000

III. *Vacations*

A. *Problem:*
Listed below are the basic data regarding the vacation program
contained in your current contract. Figure out the cost of this
contract provision in cents per hour. Assume each employee
works an average of 2,000 hours per year.

vacation time	number of employees	average hourly wage
1 week (40 hrs)	23	$4.50
2 weeks (80 hrs)	85	$4.70
3 weeks (120 hrs)	35	$4.75
4 weeks (160 hrs)	10	$4.90

Benefits Applying to a Fraction of the Membership

A. *General Formula:*
1. Figure the cents-per-hour cost of the benefit as though all of
the membership received it.
2. Multiply the above cents-per-hour cost figure by the percent of
employees that do receive this benefit.

B. *Example:*
Cost of 10% night-shift premium
Data: average hourly wage = $5.50
Percent of employees receiving shift premium = 15%
1. Cost per hour if 100% received premium = $5.50 × 10% =
$.55
2. Actual cost = $.55 × .15 = $.083

George Meany Center for Labor Studies
August 1983

Appendix M.   Sample Language on Joint Control of Pension Plan Administration and Investment

Administration

Allocation of Responsibility Among Fiduciaries for Plan and Trust Administration. The Board,* Committee, Administrator, and Trustee shall be "Named Fiduciaries" within the meaning of Section 402(a)(2) of ERISA. The Named Fiduciaries shall have only those specific powers, duties, responsibilities, and obligations as are specifically given them under this Plan or the trust agreement. In general the Board shall have the sole authority to appoint and remove the Plan Administrator and to amend or terminate the Plan in whole or in part pursuant to Sections 7.01 and 7.02 hereof. The Committee shall be responsible for the general administration of the Plan, for appointing and removing any investment managers, for monitoring the performance of any investment managers, for determining a funding policy and investment objectives for the Plan, and for determining any benefit claims appeals. The Administrator shall have the responsibility for the administration of this Plan, which responsibility is specifically described in this Plan. The Trustee shall have the sole responsibility for the administration of the trust agreement and the management of the assets held thereunder, except to the extent such responsibility is delegated to any investment managers in accordance with such trust agreement. Each Named Fiduciary may rely upon any direction, information, or action of any other Named Fiduciary as being proper, and is not required to inquire into the propriety of any such direction, information, or action. It is intended under this Plan that each Named Fiduciary shall be responsible for the proper exercise of his own powers, duties, responsibilities, and obligations under this Plan and shall not be responsible for any act or failure to act of another Named Fiduciary. An individual may serve in more than one fiduciary capacity hereunder.

Administrative Committee. (a) The general responsibility for carrying out the provisions of the Plan shall be placed in an Administrative Committee ("Committee") of not less than two employees of the Company or any affiliate thereof appointed from time to time, one by the Company and one by the Union. The Company and/or the Union may appoint more than one employee but for purposes of determining Committee decisions, all Company members shall have one aggregate vote and all Union members shall have one aggregate vote. In the event of a deadlock, a third party arbitrator shall be selected pursuant to the procedures indicated in Article VI paragraph 133 of the Basic Agreement or any successor provision thereto. The Committee may appoint from its number such officers and/or subcommittees with such powers as it shall determine and may authorize one or more

---

*"The Board" in this example is the employer.

of its number or any agent to execute or deliver any instrument or make any payment on its behalf. The Committee may designate and allocate any fiduciary responsibility to one or more of its members or to any other person or persons. It may retain counsel, employ agents, and provide for clerical, accounting, and actuarial services as it may require. The foregoing sentence shall in no way affect the duty and obligation of the Administrator to retain such services in connection with the carrying out of his duties and to designate an enrolled actuary and independent, qualified public accountant as provided in Section 5.05 hereof.

(b) The Committee shall hold meetings upon such notice, at such place, and at such times as it may from time to time determine. A meeting may be held in any manner as may be determined by the Committee, but in any event, where all members are not physically present, the actions of the Committee shall be reduced to writing and sent to all members within ten (10) days of the date of such meeting.

(c) A Company member and a Union member of the Committee shall constitute a quorum, and any action which the Plan authorizes or requires the Committee to take shall require the written approval or the affirmative vote of a majority of the Company members and a majority of the Union members.

(d) Members of the Committee shall not be paid any compensation from the assets of the Plan.

(e) Subject to the provisions of the Plan, the Committee may from time to time establish rules for the transaction of its business. The determination of the Committee as to any disputed question pertaining to the Plan shall be conclusive.

(f) Any member of the Committee may resign by delivering his written resignation to the Company or Union which appointed him. Any member of the Committee may be removed by the Company or Union which appointed him, and such removal shall be effective at such time as is provided for by such entity. Notice of such removal shall be conveyed to the member so removed.

(g) In addition, the Committee shall have the following specific duties and responsibilities under the Plan:

(i) To determine a funding policy and investment objectives in accordance with Section 6.02 herein; provided, however, that in accomplishing the foregoing, the Committee shall not be deemed to be superseding, restricting, or otherwise modifying the exclusive investment authority and discretion that may have been delegated to the Trustee or any investment managers;

(ii) To adopt such procedures as the Committee may deem appropriate and advisable to monitor and review the performance of any investment managers so as to determine whether the Plan assets have been managed in accordance with the funding policy and objectives established by the Committee and with the requirements relating to the fiduciary duties and responsibilities to exercise prudence, to diversify investment of Plan assets, and to refrain from engaging in certain "prohibited transactions" that are detailed in ERISA;

(iii) To obtain such periodic written reports or other accounting as the Committee may desire from such investment managers in regard to the performance of their respective delegated duties and responsibilities and to meet semiannually, or at such other intervals as the Committee may determine, with such investment managers for the purpose of reviewing and evaluating such reports or other accountings with them; and

(iv) To prepare a written report with respect to the Committee's review and evaluation of the performance of such investment managers, including therein any findings and conclusions of the Committee concerning the propriety and/or advisability of either retaining or removing and replacing any such investment manager, such report to be made at least annually and at such other time that the Committee deems necessary and advisable.

Glossary

Actuarial adjustments for gain or loss. Periodical modifications in the annual contribution rate to compensate for variances from actuarial assumptions.

Actuarial assumptions. Estimates regarding future events that the actuary must make in order to predict the cost of providing a certain retirement income.

Actuarial reduction. The reduction in the normal retirement benefit which offsets a cost increase to the plan when a participant retires ahead of schedule.

Actuarial report. An actuary's report to the company recommending how much to contribute yearly to the pension fund to fund promised benefits.

Actuary. Someone licensed to compute insurance risks.

Age and service vesting. See *Rule of 45.*

Annuity. A promise to make periodic payments to a designated person for a designated period of time. See also *Refund annuity, Life annuities certain and continuous.*

Cliff vesting. Full (100 percent) vesting after *x* years of service, but with no gradation of eligibility before that time.

Deferred vested pension. The normal or early retirement pension provided to vested participants who separate from service before the date they are eligible for early retirement.

Defined-Benefit pension. A pension that contains a specific promise of how much a retired member will receive per month or per year.

Defined-Contribution pension. A pension that specifies only the amount to be contributed to the plan.

Elapsed time method of service counting. A method for determining a workers' time in service by subtracting the hire-in date from the termination date.

Employee Retirement Income Security Act (ERISA). Legislation passed in 1974 that set minimum pension standards.

ERISAfication. A change in a pension plan to bring it into line with amendments to ERISA.

Fiduciary. Anyone who exercises discretionary control over the operation of a pension plan and its assets.

Flat dollar and service benefit formula. A retirement benefit formula based on years of service times a specific dollar multiplier, such as $10 per month per year of service.

Flat dollar benefit formula. A retirement benefit formula which calls for a specific pension amount without regard to income or service.

Fund earnings. Earnings that return to the pension trust fund for reinvestment or payment of benefits.

Funding. The process of setting aside money on a systematic basis to pay retirement benefits.

Graded vesting. A vesting schedule that calls for partial vesting, say 50 percent, after a specific length of service. The vested portion is increased each year until it reaches 100 percent.

Hours counting method of service calculation. A service counting rule that requires a certain number of hours to be credited during a 12-month period for a participant to be credited with one year of service toward vesting, benefit eligibility, or benefit calculation.

Income and service benefit formula. A retirement benefit formula based on income and credited service, such as 1 percent of average annual income multiplied by the years of service.

Income-Based benefit formula. A retirement formula based solely on income, such as 50 percent of the final yearly salary.

Individual retirement account. A do-it-yourself retirement plan available to all wage earners and spouses; also known as an IRA. An IRA permits, subject to Internal Revenue Service guidelines, deferral of taxes on the money put aside until the money is withdrawn at retirement.

Inland Steel decision. A 1948 ruling of the National Labor Relations Board that pensions are included in the National Labor Relations Act provision requiring companies to bargain with unions over wages, hours, and other conditions of employment.

IRA. See *Individual retirement account.*

Joint and survivor coverage. Payment of the pension benefit to the participant and spouse until both die. After the death of the participant, the spouse receives a percentage of the participant's pension, usually one half or two thirds.

Keogh plan. A government-approved individual retirement savings plan for the self-employed, similar to an IRA.

Life annuities certain and continuous. An annuity guaranteeing a certain number of monthly payments regardless of whether the participant lives or dies, with the promise that the payments will continue for life.

Parity rule. A break-in-service rule that says a participant loses pension rights if the break in service exceeds the length of time worked.

Participant. An individual who is accruing or maintaining rights under a pension plan.

PBGC. See *Pension Benefit Guaranty Corp.*

Pension. A group savings plan that has the exclusive purpose of providing a secure retirement income for those who leave the work force because of age.

Pension and Welfare Plan Disclosure Act. A 1958 law requiring companies to file certain pension information with the Department of Labor.

Pension Benefit Guaranty Corporation (PBGC). A nonprofit organization established by ERISA to provide basic minimum insurance against the loss of pension benefits in the event of a pension plan termination.

Portability. The ability to transfer accumulated pension benefits from one plan to another when a worker changes jobs.

Preretirement surviving spouse benefit. A benefit which provides that if the participant dies while actively employed, the spouse will receive 50 percent of the pension calculated as though the employee had retired the day death occurred. This benefit is required under REACT at time of vesting.

Qualified pension plan. A tax-qualified pension plan approved by the Internal Revenue Service. "Tax-qualified" means the company can take a tax deduction for its contributions to the pension plan.

Refund annuity. An annuity that guarantees a return to the surviving spouse of the unused portion of the purchase price or value of the annuity.

Retirement Equity Act of 1984 (REACT). A federal law that amended ERISA with the purpose of providing greater pension equity for women workers and surviving spouses.

Rule of 45. An ERISA vesting formula which provides that a participant with five years of service and whose age plus five years equals 45 or more will be partially vested.

Summary plan description. A summary of the provisions of a pension plan.

Surviving spouse benefit. Payments to the spouse of a deceased participant.

Thirty-And-Out. A retirement option that permits retirement after 30 years' credited service, regardless of age.

Thirty-Year cap. Accumulation of pension service up to and including the 30th year of service, at which point the accumulation of pension service is frozen.

Three-Legged stool. The theory that a combination of an individual's savings, Social Security, and a private pension will provide secure retirement income.

Time preference. Preferring income in the present rather than deferring it to the future.

Trustee. One responsible for managing the assets of a pension fund in the best interests of the participants.

Turnover discount. A savings to the plan that results from employee turnover.

Vesting. The right to terminate service at some point in the worklife without endangering pension benefits that have accumulated to that point. See also *Cliff vesting, Graded vesting, Rule of 45.*

Index

A

Actuarial
  adjustments   11
  assumptions   31, 141, 159-161
  reduction   50-54, 140
  report   11, 85
Actuary   10-11
Administration (*see also* Investment,
      control; Investment, joint
      control)   61, 144
  joint administrative
      committee   73-74
Administrator   18
Age   35-36, 61-62
  effect on cost   28, 152
Age and service vesting   70-71, 143,
      145, 146
Allied Chemical and Alkali Workers v.
      Pittsburgh Plate Glass
      Co.   14
Amendment (*see* Modification of plan)
Annual earnings   46
Annuity   57-59
Annuity Tables   150, 151
Arbitration   73
Assets   141

B

Bargaining (*see* Negotiations)
Beneficiary   11
Benefit
  accumulation   65, 145
  calculations 24-33, 40, 44-45, 47-49
  eligibility   65, 71-72
  formulas   24-33, 44-50
  improvements   13
  rules   61

Benefits   4, 10, 12, 13, 22, 23
  basic   43, 87
  early retirement   43, 50, 51-54, 140
  flat dollar   50
  fringe   174-177
  normal retirement   43-50, 87
  surviving spouse   43, 55-58
Bracketing   48
Break-in-service   67-68
  rules   61
Brown v. Arizona   53

C

Calculations (*see also* Formulas)
  actuarial reduction   51-52
  costs of plan   102-118
  early retirement   51
  preretirement surviving spouse
      coverage   56, 118
  retirement benefit   24-33, 40,
      44-45, 47-49
  service   72
Career average plan   45-46
Cliff vesting   69-70
  comparison with graded vesting   70
COLA (*see* Cost-of-living adjustment)
Collective bargaining   2, 74
Committee   72-74, 126
Company
  contributions   12, 84-85, 146-147
  liability   18-19
Contract   2-3
  defined-benefit (*see also* Defined-
      benefit pension
      contract)   9
  defined-contribution (*see also*
      Defined-contribution
      pension contract)   9
  qualified pension plan   9-10

Cost-of-living adjustment 45, 47
Cost impact of plan 119-121
   cents-per-hour 102-104
   current benefits 102
   disability pensions 115-116
   early retirement 110-115
   fringe benefits 174-177
   improvements 105-108
   interpretation 105
   percent of earnings
         formula 108-110
   trends 102-104
   variables 107
   vesting 116-117

D

Deferred vested pension 66
Defined-benefit pension contract (*see
    also* Negotiated pension
    plan, advantages) 9, 32-33,
    41, 149
   age 61-62
   bargaining agenda 143-146
   benefit eligibility 71-72
   benefits 43-59, 87
   break-in-service 68
   comparison with defined-
      contribution
      pension 35-41, 75
   disability 40, 43
   elapsed time method 63, 68
   formulas 44-50
   funding 74-76
   group account 36
   hours counting method 65-68
   language 60-78, 87-88
   leave of absence 63, 64, 69
   modification of plan 17, 61, 76-77
   past service 40
   risk 39
   service accrual 62-63
   vesting 65, 68-71
Defined-contribution pension contract
    (*see also* Negotiated pension
    plan) 9
   age 35-36
   bargaining agenda 146-147
   comparison with defined-benefit
      pension 35-41, 75
   definition 34
   disability 40
   disadvantages 38-42
   individual account 36

   interest rate 38
   past service 40
   piggyback plans 42
   risk 39
Definitions 16-17
Department of Labor (*see also* Forms,
    DOL 5500) 73
Disability
   flat dollar benefits 50
   short-term 65, 68
   pensions 115-116, 145, 146
Dispute resolution 17-18, 72-73, 144
Documentation 15
DOL (*see* Department of Labor)

E

Early retirement 17, 144
   actuarial reduction 50-54
   benefits 43, 50, 51-54, 140
   costs 110-115
   health insurance 54
   preretirement surviving spouse
      coverage 55-57, 117-118,
      140
   social security supplement 54
Economics of plan 97
Economy 6-7, 47
   inflation 49
Elapsed time method 63-65
Employee Retirement Income
      Security Act of 1974 15-19,
      40-41
   age 62
   age and service vesting (Rule of
      45) 70
   break-in-service 68
   dispute resolution 73
   elapsed time method 62
   funding 74-75
   hours-counting method 62, 65-67,
      147
   modification of plan 61
   National Labor Relations Act of
      1935 75
   service accrual 62, 64
   surviving spouse coverage 55-59
   termination 137
Employee rights 18
Employer contributions 12, 84-85,
    146-147
ERISA (*See* Employee Retirement
    Income Security Act of 1974)

F

Federal government
   National Labor Relations Act of
      1935   12-15
   pension administration   8-19
Fiduciary   127-128
50 percent surviving spouse
      option   44, 59
Final five-year average plan   45-46
Flat dollar benefit   50
Flat dollar and service formula   48
Forms
   D-2   18
   DOL 5500   18, 77, 85-86, 104-105,
      162-171
Formulas
   benefit   24-33, 44-50, 174-177
   flat dollar   50
   flat dollar and service   48
   income based   44
   income and service   44-49
   percentage of earnings   108-110
Fund earnings   11, 149
Funding   10, 22, 61, 74
   funding waivers   75, 145
Future service only provision   49

G

Good faith bargaining   15
Government (see Federal government)
Graded vesting
   comparisons   70
   5-to-15 year grading   69-70
   5-to-10 year grading   69-70

H

Health insurance   54
Hours counting method   65-67
   layoffs   67
Hours, defined   66
Hybrid plans   41

I

Income and service formulas   44-49
Income-based formulas   44
Individual funding   37

advantages   37-38
disadvantages   38-40
Inflation   49
Inland Steel v. Local 1010, United
      Steelworkers   12
Insurance carriers   141-142
Internal Revenue Service   9
   funding waiver   75, 145
   qualified pension plan   79-80
   tax benefits   9, 75
Interest rate   26-28, 38, 150, 151
Investment
   control   122-123, 126-128
   joint control   124-125, 129-131, 146
   options   11
IRS (see Internal Revenue Service)

J

Job turnover   31-33
Joint administrative committee   72-74
Joint-and-survivor coverage   57-59
Joint investment control   124-125,
      129-131, 178-180

L

Language (see also Rules;
            Negotiations, language)
   defined-benefit plan   60-78
Layoff   67, 141
Leave of absence   63, 64
   layoff   67, 141
   long-term   67
vesting   69
Legislation (See Employee Retirement
            Income Security Act of 1974;
            National Labor Relations Act
            of 1935; Pension and Welfare
            Plan Disclosure Act of 1958;
            Retirement Equity Act of
            1984)
Life annuities certain and
      continuous   59
Life expectancy   25

M

Mandatory bargaining   12-13, 14-15
Modification of plan   17, 61, 76-77
Mortality tables   31-33, 153-154, 155
Multiplier   45, 47-49

N

National Labor Relations Act of
        1935   12-15, 75, 82
National Labor Relations Board   12,
        82
Negative earnings   11
Negative return on investment   11
Negotiated pension plan   1, 9, 25, 41,
        66, 97
  administration   8-19, 61, 178-180
  advantages   4, 20-21
  articles   9-10
  benefit formulas   24-33, 44-50
  benefits   4, 10, 13, 23, 43-59, 87
  committee   126
  costs   101-121, 152, 155
  definition   20, 21
  disadvantages   21
  fiduciary   127-128
  funding   (see Funding)
  governmental role   8-19
  group aspects   29-30
  improvements   13, 105-108
  interest rate   26-28
  investment control   122-131
  mandatory bargaining   12-14
  mortality   30-33
  participation   61-62
  plant closing   132-142, 146
  qualified pension plan   9-10, 79-80
  reporting services   88-89
  sample plan   24-25
  termination   134-139, 145
  turnover   30-33, 155
Negotiations   8-9, 10, 21, 22, 90
  actuarial evaluation   85
  agenda   143-147
  benefit eligibility   72
  benefits   87
  company response   135-139
  contributions   84-85
  costs   101-121
  disability program   145, 147
  dispute resolution   72-73
  expiration of contract   98-99
  first day   93-96
  funding   74, 75
  information   80-89, 133-134, 158
  investment   76, 122-131
  joint administrative
        committee   72-74
  language   88, 96-97, 125-126,
        129-131, 133, 135
  layoffs   67, 144, 146, 147
  long-term agreement   48-49

  mandatory   12-13
  plan participants   83-84
  plant closing   132-142, 146
  preparation   79-89, 91-93, 127-128
  preretirement surviving spouse
        coverage   56-57, 117-118
  proposals   91-93, 97-98, 139-142
  ratification meeting   99-100
  retirement   59, 84
  service accrual   63
  strategy   128-131
  timeline   90-100
  union rights   77-78
NLRA (see National Labor Relations
        Act of 1935)
NLRB (see National Labor Relations
        Board)
Normal retirement benefit   44-50

P

Parity rule   68
Participation   16, 143, 146
  rules   61
PBGC (See Pension Benefit Guaranty
        Corporation)
Pension and Welfare Plan Disclosure
        Act of 1958   18
Pension Benefit Guaranty
        Corporation   19, 135, 137,
        139
Pensions (see Negotiated pension plan)
Permissive bargaining   14-15
Plan administrator   18
Plant closing   132-142, 146
Preretirement surviving spouse
        benefit   43, 55-57
  cost impact   117-118
Proposal preparation   91-93, 139-142
Pure life annuities   44

Q

Qualified pension plan   79-80

R

REACT (see Retirement Equity Act of
        1984)
Refund annuities   59
Reporting services   88-89
Retirement Equity Act of 1984   16,
        17, 43-44, 144-145
  break-in-service   68
  surviving spouse coverage   57

Retirement income   3-4, 23-24
Retirement income plan (*see*
        Negotiated pension plan)
Rules
    benefit eligibility   61
    break-in-service   61
    parity   68
    participation   61
    Rule of 45   70
    service counting   61, 64
    vesting   61

S

Savings   3
Security, economic   2-3, 23-24
Service accrual   62-68, 145
Service counting rules   61, 64
Severance from service   67-68
Sex segregation   53-54
Social security   3-4
    supplement   54-55
Spousal coverage   17, 43-44
    surviving spouse benefits (*see also*
        Preretirement surviving
        spouse benefit)   55-59
Standard benefits   43
Summary plan description   9
Survivor option   17, 55

T

Tax benefits   9, 19
Termination   17, 134-139, 145
30-and-out program   5, 54-55
30-year-cap   5-6

Time preference   4
Trustee   11-12
    reports   86
Turnover discounts   71
Turnover tables   31-33, 155

U

Union
    benefits   87
    interest in investment
        control   124-125, 146
    leadership   4
    plant closing   132-134
    rights   77-78

V

Vesting   16, 18, 62, 68
    age and service   70-71, 143, 145,
        146
    cliff   69
    cost impact   116-117
    graded   69-70
    rules   61
    service standard   65, 144
    10-year   38
    turnover discounts   71
    20-year   38

W

Wagner Act (*see* National Labor
        Relations Act of 1935)
Women   53